THE

CORRS

THE UNOFFICIAL BOOK

THE
CORRS

jane cornwell

Virgin

First published in 1999 by Virgin Books
an imprint of Virgin Publishing Ltd
Thames Wharf Studios
Rainville Road
London W6 9HT

A catalogue record for this book is available from the British Library

ISBN 185227 840 4

Printed and bound in Great Britain by Jarrold Books

Reproduction by Digital Generation Ltd.

Designed by Slatter~Anderson

PICTURE CREDITS

ALL ACTION
Corlouer 48, 118; Dave Hogan 5 (top), 41, 50, 54, 76, 78, 108; Paul Meaker 2, 52, 91, 93, 111, 112; Suzan Moore 30, 31, 53, 80, 81, 104; Justin Thomas 9, 42, 92, 94, 106, 107, 122

FAMOUS
Fred Duval 67; Simon Guy 15, 39, 62, 63

LFI
David Fisher 7, 8, 57, 86, 114, 115, 116; Awais Butt 114

REDFERNS
Patrick Ford 1, 3, 5 (bottom), 12, 16, 19, 21, 25, 32, 37, 59, 71, 72, 86, 88, 90, 96, 100, 103, 119, 124, 127; Nicky J. Sims 5 (centre bottom), 6, 43, 44, 79, 84, 89, 95, 109, 120, 121; Ebet Roberts 18, 66, 70, 73, 75, 98, 103; Mick Hutson 28, 61; Pete Cronin 60; Garry Brandon 64; Leon Morris 65; Val Wilmer 68

REX
Brian Rasic 5 (centre top), 17, 74, 83, 87, 97, 102, 110; Warren Johnson 10, 11, 22; Ken McKay 20, 26, 35, 46, 56, 77; RC 36; HMA 49; Charles Ommanney 38; Hayley Madder 117; Dennis Stone 123

STARFILE
Max Goldstein 27, 113

The Publishers would like to thank the following for their permission to use quotes in the book:
Hot Press Magazine 43, 69, 94, 105
Sky Magazine 34, 55
Q Magazine 85

Contents

Introducing the Family

The Corrs are one of Ireland's most successful musical exports. A multi-million selling international phenomenon, this quartet of three sisters and a brother blend the best of traditional Irish folk music with unforgettable pop melodies, acknowledging their ancestral roots while embracing modern rhythms and technology. The Corrs give the tin whistle, the violin and the hand-held drum called a bodhrán as much emphasis as synthesisers, keyboards and electric guitar. Aided by crystal clear voices and celestial harmonies, they weave Celtic melodies into every track.

The result is inspirational and optimistic, passionate and highly accessible. You *could* call them a traditional Irish pop-rock band, if there was such a thing. Despite their huge commercial success, The Corrs have never written songs with any particular market in mind, and their music crosses boundaries and defies categorisation as a consequence, as does their appeal.

The Corrs are beloved of all age groups. Their youthful enthusiasm and easy confidence have won over live audiences everywhere, from Sweden to Japan, from Spain to Australia. Their fans include children and grandparents, Irish patriots and pop lovers; anyone with a love of sweet voices, straight-to-the-point songs and stirring instrumentals. Their fans are loyal, and usually restrained – although the Garda (Irish police) have been known to rescue them from over-zealous autograph hunters at concerts back home.

Ireland's premier pop family has a synergy that could only come from growing up under one roof. Sibling rivalry seems to be virtually non-existent, and tensions rare.

Refreshingly down to earth, she is intent on making the most of fame while it lasts

Indeed, given the sisters' slim physiques, doe eyes and identical cheekbones, it's been easy for some to see them as merely a homogenous whole. But each of them is, of course, an individual, with an individual's traits and idiosyncrasies. They have all stated that The Corrs is more than the sum of its parts, and that they could never continue as a band if one of them decided to leave.

Tall and chiselled Jim (b.1964), the band's keyboard player and guitarist, is the eldest and most laid-back member. As befits a man with three such photogenic sisters, he is happy to take a back seat in interviews and photo shoots, preferring to keep an eye firmly fixed on The Corrs' chart positions. Classically trained violinist Sharon (b.1970) is a serious musician, a woman who is influenced as much by Satie and Dvořák as she is by The

Rolling Stones. Refreshingly down to earth, she is intent on making the most of fame while it lasts.

Drummer and bodhrán player Caroline (b.1973) is the feisty tomboy of the band, a percussionist who plays in her trademark pair of black gloves. Where her sisters enjoy being made-up and styled for promotional appearances, Caroline attends the innumerable Corrs photo shoots under good humoured sufferance, for the band's sake. Striking lead singer and tin whistle player Andrea (b.1974) is The Corrs' charismatic front woman, a self-confessed romantic dreamer and the object of desire for millions of young fans.

The Corrs' unique talent was nurtured by their parents, Jean and Gerry, who captured on home video many of the band's early efforts in their bedroom-cum-studio. Formed in 1990, they came together for the first time as a band to audition for a part in Alan Parker's critically acclaimed movie *The Commitments*. Andrea won a small role as Jimmy Rabbitte's younger sister, and they so impressed John Hughes, the film's musical director, that he decided to become their manager.

In 1994, after signing to Grammy Award-winning producer David Foster's label 143 Records and recording their debut album *Forgiven, Not Forgotten*, The Corrs' bid for international recognition began in earnest. Nine times platinum in Ireland, seven times platinum in Australia, two times platinum in New Zealand, Denmark and Spain and gold in Japan, Canada, France, Norway and the UK, the album succeeded beyond the family's wildest dreams.

Their universally acclaimed follow up, 1997's *Talk On Corners*, looks set to exceed the victories of the first. Its guitar-oriented, rockier sound is both the legacy of time spent touring the world and the result of a mission to add fresh new attitude to The Corrs' sound. Their image has changed too. Andrea has defended the new sexier look the girls have adopted, reasoning that with the heat they generate on stage, it just wasn't practical to go on wearing woolly jumpers.

The group's aim remains the same. They want to keep on doing what they love – creating and performing music – and to continue making people happy while they're at it. Their music expresses and encourages a gamut of emotions; its compulsive hooks, catchy pop tunes, power ballads and instrumentals beg repeated playing. It reflects both the mystical, haunting qualities of the Irish landscape as much as it does the *joie de vivre* of Ireland's traditional culture.

As a live act, The Corrs replicate all these elements and more. Their skilful, polished performances invest each song with an added dimension, Andrea taking up her tin whistle like some angelic Pied Piper, while Sharon coaxes soaring notes from her violin or sings harmonies, her hand gestures understated versions of her youngest sister's, her manner serene. Up the back, alert and focused behind a huge drum kit, Caroline propels the band with percussive backing, occasionally dancing down the front to play a bodhrán inscribed with The Corrs' trademark Celtic signature. Jim plays keyboards with a guitar slung around his neck; then, back on guitar, moves centre stage with Sharon so that both stand playing either side of Andrea for full dramatic effect.

The Corrs love playing live. It's a reciprocal thing – the buzz they get from the crowd, they've said, reaffirms why it is they do what they do. Much attention has been centred

It makes

it easy to

get along

if you all

share the

same

dream

on the girls' photogenic features (Jim, though a handsome man, receives rather less attention), but it irks them when the media concentrate on their appearance rather than their music. The Corrs often point out that it isn't their looks that sell their records. Still, they're savvy enough to understand that aesthetics matter in the music business, and that part of their success can be attributed to sex appeal. So if their fans want a catwalk image, that's exactly what they are going to get.

On stage they are usually sleekly dressed in black. Jim likes jeans, T-shirts and long leather jackets; for more glamorous occasions his shirts might be subtly embossed with flowers. Caroline wears lycra tops and trousers; Sharon dresses with plunging necklines; Andrea black feather boas and knee-length skirts split at the thigh. Black, they say, best suits their milky Irish complexions. All the sisters favour high heels, vests with shoestring straps and eyeshadow in shades of grey, green and gold. For their 1998 St Patrick's Day concert at the Royal Albert Hall in London, their black outfits were subtly woven with fibres that glittered – a classic look, with a Corrs twist.

The Corrs' camera-friendly visages are a marketing department's dream; they have been groomed for magazine shoots the world over. In one magazine they were dressed like Helmut Newton models, in black tuxedos with severe, gelled hairstyles; in another as ethereal Irish maidens in white chiffon (Jim, of course, excepted). They say it's similar to the way they used to play at dressing up as children, but they have also admitted that long, drawn-out photo shoots can play havoc with one's sense of self.

The Corrs haven't succumbed to the rock'n'roll lifestyle which affects many of their peers. Unfailingly professional, they come across as the most 'normal' band in the world. They do, however, have a penchant for champagne, and between them have been known to sink up to three bottles at a time. The girls are also fond of wine-soaked late lunches on their rare days off.

An abundance of talent is one thing (and The Corrs certainly aren't lacking in that direction), but a lot of hard work is required to guarantee album sales. Ambitious from the start, the band have become dab hands at promoting themselves through TV, radio and print interviews, in-store appearances and touring. They will often visit up to four continents in three weeks, and have toured almost constantly for three years. Long days are de rigeur, lie-ins a luxury.

Their record label calls them 'the hardest working band in showbiz.' Their manager John Hughes agrees. He has said that his charges achieved more in one year than most performers achieve in seven. It hasn't been easy but The Corrs' tenacity has paid off. After all, who could fail to be seduced by such a package?

One downside of spending so much time on the road is the effect that it has had on their personal lives. Both Sharon and Caroline are in relationships, which they work hard at maintaining in spite of long separations – the band's phone bills are gigantic as a result.

Jim and Andrea are single and 'still looking.' All The Corrs have commented that the pressures of fame, not to mention the tightly-knit nature of the group, make it difficult to meet prospective partners. It's the price you pay for success, they shrug. All of them hanker after marriage and babies at some point in the future, but for the time being their philosophy is 'all for one, and one for all.'

This rapport has also produced many of their collectively written songs. Each song is generally a collaborative affair. Depending on who is inspired first, one of them might pen some lyrics and leave the others to add the tune. Or two of them may write together, or the music may come first. Their aim is first to write a good pop or rock song; then, via a process of trial and error, apply a traditional arrangement to it. It's an organic process they are determined to maintain. Themes are broad, encompassing love lost, found and unrequited; life, tragedy, hope, dreams and fantasy. Andrea took on a bigger role for *Talk On Corners*, writing or co-writing almost all of the lyrics with a number of renowned studio hitmakers.

Given that they often spend up to fifteen hours a day, seven days a week in each other's company, it would be unusual if tensions didn't surface from time to time. But each was raised to be mature and give each other space. The Corrs' strength is that they

The story of how they have got to where they are today is a fascinating one; a testimony to self-belief, perseverance and sheer unadulterated talent

are a family with a team attitude, one which has helped them deflect the knockbacks they initially received from American record companies. They've said that seeing the same faces every day would make anybody go a bit crazy. They have even started to speak their own private language, which can be confusing for anyone else on the tour bus. But, as they've also said, it makes it easy to get along if you all share the same dream. It also helps that, these days, they all request their own hotel rooms.

Having learned from a previous punishing touring schedule which at one point saw the band come down with a collective case of flu, The Corrs are also learning to relax again. 'We tried to do the whole world at once and we nearly killed ourselves,' Andrea told *Vox* Magazine. 'We wouldn't want to change what we did, but never again...'

The Corrs have their hearts and minds set on reaching increasing numbers of people with their music. The story of how they have got to where they are today is a fascinating one; a testimony to self-belief, perseverance and sheer unadulterated talent. With, it must be said, a bit of Irish luck thrown in for good measure. From their humble beginnings around the family piano in Dundalk to singing for the Pope at the Vatican; from auditioning for *The Commitments* to opening for the likes of Celine Dion and The Rolling Stones, it has been an exhilarating journey for The Corrs.

A MUSICAL UPBRINGING

At first glance, not a lot goes on in Dundalk. A County Louth harbour town situated halfway between Dublin and Belfast, 13 kilometres from the border, it was infamous as a Republican stronghold during the Troubles, and boasts a neo-Gothic courthouse and the tallest windmill in Ireland among its rather limited attractions. Its 35,000 or so inhabitants are affable, welcoming people who enjoy the odd pint of Guinness in the town's many pubs. There they can be found tapping their feet along to any of the excellent cover bands or live traditional music sessions, revelling in the convivial atmosphere commonly known as *craic* ('crack'), and even joining in the sessions if they feel so inclined. Like so many places in Ireland, music is Dundalk's lifeblood.

The Corrs were born into music. For twenty years their parents, Jean (b.1942), a housewife, and Gerry (b.1932), a retired Electricity Board employee, played ballads and folk tunes in local bands. During their offspring's formative years they founded their own showband, with Jean singing and Gerry playing keyboards. They covered hits by such melody-oriented outfits as Abba, The Eagles, Fleetwood Mac, Simon and Garfunkel and The Carpenters. Both have recently retired from the Dundalk/Dublin music circuit, although Gerry still plays the organ in Dundalk's Redeemer Church every Sunday.

The four children travelled to gigs with their parents in the family estate car. At the time, not knowing any other way of life, they thought it was what everybody's parents did. Jean and Gerry encouraged their children's musical talents, in the first instance by teaching them how to play the family piano and later, aided by professionals, other instruments. Gerry, a staunch Catholic and firm-but-fair disciplinarian, is fond of joking

that it appears as if these lessons have finally paid off.

The Corrs maintain that they were never pressured into performing, in the way that the Osmonds or the Jackson Five allegedly were. Neither did they grow up in a hillbilly household, playing around a bonfire with goats and cows peering over their shoulders, as befits the stereotype of a 'family' band. For them, music has always been a pleasure and a gift, and never a chore. Their modest home harboured nothing more than four ambitious kids, two doting parents, a dog named Judy and a love of music that became all encompassing. The Corrs often joke that if there were another sibling, who was tone deaf and couldn't play an instrument, things would be very difficult for them indeed. A long-lost cousin, Gerard Cox from Coalisland, County Tyrone, did approach them after a Belfast concert in May 1996, but there are no plans for a collaboration!

It was always the Corrs' intention to form a band. Given their musical upbringing and surroundings, there was never really anything else that any of them wanted to do. Their disciplined work ethic is undoubtedly a legacy of their upbringing. On a school night, for example, they were instructed to be home by six; there was also a curfew at weekends. Gerry, a small, trim man with a beard and oversize glasses, is still very much the head of the household. The words 'Time for bed!', however tongue-in-cheek the delivery, can still send his grown-up children scurrying upstairs. Equally, he has passed on his faith: Sharon, Caroline and Andrea attended mass until they were 18, Jim up until his early teens. All speak happily of a relaxed and liberal childhood, though the girls admit that 'Mammy' – as they call their handsome, raven-haired mother – would prefer they were still *au naturel*, with uncut hair, unshaven legs and unplucked eyebrows.

Jean and Gerry are immensely proud of their children. They might be able to play The Corrs' songs with their eyes shut and recite the lyrics verbatim, but the success of Jim, Sharon, Caroline and Andrea remains incredibly exciting. The Corrs Senior admit that though they knew their children would make it, they never imagined that they would scale such dizzying heights. They are confident that their kids are level-headed enough to control their success, rather than let their success control them. Both parents read every interview and record every television programme they can get their hands on, and they always get a buzz of excitement whenever a Corrs song comes on the radio.

THE CORRS WERE BORN INTO MUSIC

The huge success of the band has meant long periods away from Dundalk; Jean has commented that often the only time she gets to see her children these days is on the television. With The Corrs' time at home increasingly limited by the demands of touring, they have partially solved the problem by flying their parents out to meet them. On one occasion, just as Jean and Gerry were about to hop on a plane to visit The Corrs in Denmark, they realised they'd forgotten their passports and had to head back to Dundalk. The Corrs compensated with a trip to the golden beaches of Australia, now one of their favourite destinations.

When not rehearsing, playing or touring, The Corrs love to walk in the beautiful countryside surrounding Dundalk, or simply catch up with close friends. They'll have people over for dinner, where conversation will range from books and films to religion and politics. In the public eye, however, they tend to abide by John Hughes' maxim that sex, politics and religion are private matters, and rarely discuss these subjects in interviews.

While emphatically not a political band – somewhat controversially, they consider music and politics diametrically opposed – they are, like everyone else, frustrated by Ireland's Troubles, despite the recent peace agreement. Borders, they point out, can't be seen from satellites. They have played on a number of bills for Irish peace causes – they even organised a special benefit concert on RTE's *Late Late Show* for the victims of the Omagh bomb blast – but would prefer to keep their political opinions to themselves. At the end of the day, The Corrs are all about entertainment.

It has always been thus. When Gerry's father gave him the big upright piano from his house as a wedding present, Jean and Gerry initially left it in their cramped sitting room. When, pushed for space, they hired six men to shift it upstairs, it was to the room that would eventually become Jim's bedroom. There it remained. Jean remembers Jim playing when he could barely reach the keys. One by one, his sisters followed suit, and plenty of arguments ensued over whose turn it was. Perhaps to smooth things over and add a bit of variety, Gerry invited their fiddle-playing local priest over to teach the instrument to three-year-old Caroline. Caroline, however, was so terrified by this large man in black that he moved on to six-year-old Sharon instead, who took to the violin like the proverbial duck to water.

Inspired by the mix of Irish folk and American pop music they heard around them, the teenage Corrs became a band in the privacy of Jim's bedroom, in a house he'd rented around the corner. Teenagers in bedrooms the world over have always had a go at being pop stars, but this lot had real instruments instead of tennis rackets, and real microphones instead of hairbrushes. They even had a little eight-track recording desk. Andrea sang lead vocals, Sharon fiddled, and both Caroline and Jim played keyboards. They covered songs like 'Knock On Wood', swivelled their hips in front of the mirror, laughed and played up to their parents' video camera. On Thursday nights they would gather religiously around the television set to watch BBC TV's *Top of the Pops*. Jean would often scribble down the lyrics so she could sing them at her and Gerry's next gig.

Music has always dominated their lives. Jim, a guitarist as well as a pianist, briefly attended music college before struggling along as a session musician with a variety of Dublin bands. He'd rented a cream-coloured, two-storey house around the corner from

his parents' place on the comfortable Ard Easmunn estate, and kitted out a dank back bedroom as a studio. Sharon worked in different orchestras, managed a record shop and had begun playing the odd traditional music gig with Jim, often at their aunt's pub, *McManus's*. His long-haired sisters Caroline and Andrea were still attending the local Dun Lughaidh Convent, but all would gather around at Jim's to practise their stab at world domination. Jim began to dream of family rock success. The question was, of course, how to go about getting it. The only time they had played in public before was when their relatives persuaded them to do so on Christmas Day.

The answer arrived on June 14 1990, in the form of auditions for Alan Parker's film of Roddy Doyle's book *The Commitments*. This was a bright, energetic, BAFTA award-winning hit about a North Dublin soul band who triumph over adversity and transcend the despair of their surroundings. In a case of life imitating art, it's easy to imagine The Corrs among the long line of hopefuls standing forlornly outside Commitments manager Jimmy Rabbitte's house.

After some heavy-duty rehearsing, Jim rounded up 16-year-old Andrea and the rest of his siblings and hotfooted the 93 kilometres from Dundalk to The Waterfront in Dublin to compete alongside hundreds of other hopefuls. The Corr family had become The Corrs.

Jim began to dream of family rock success. The question was, of course, how to go about getting it

Understandably nervous, they did two covers – 'Quincy Jones' and 'Knock on Wood' – and read prepared pieces in front of Alan Parker himself. As a result, Jim, Sharon and Caroline won themselves the grand sum of £20 a day as extras. Their parts were so small that spotting Caroline anywhere in the film has become something of a sport for Corrs fans.

Footage of Andrea at the *Commitments* auditions shows a pretty, composed young woman, twirling a strand of long, permed hair around a finger and answering questions with a self-possession beyond her age. Casting director Ros Hubbard was so impressed that she cast this youngest Corr (who had already acted in a number of amateur plays in Dundalk) in a small speaking role as Jimmy Rabbitte's feisty, epithet-muttering little sister, Sharon. Her brief filmic highlights included blow-drying her hair in the mirror and leaning moodily on the shoulder of her screen brother, played by Robert Arkins.

Ros Hubbard then rang the film's musical advisor John Hughes, an erstwhile musician and friend of *Riverdance* supremo Bill Whelan. She told him that he simply *had* to manage this multi-talented quartet. Hughes wasn't one hundred per cent sure if he wanted to be a manager. Neither was he certain that all of the Corrs were cut out to be in a band. He decided to give them a go nevertheless, and hopped on a train to Dundalk, where Jim met him at the station and suggested they go and pick up the girls. As they parked outside the Dun Lughaidh Convent, two schoolgirls in green uniforms came out to meet them, schoolbags slung over their shoulders. It was Caroline and Andrea. Hughes has said that when he considered band managing, this wasn't exactly what he had in mind.

Still, as Bill Whelan maintains, The Corrs' distinctive sound was right there from their earliest demos. Impressed by their talent and maturity, Hughes agreed to come on board – and hatched a ten-year plan for success. And why not? The Corrs were the real deal. The girls looked gorgeous, Jim was equally handsome (after losing an unflattering spiky haircut), they wrote finely crafted songs, played their own instruments and harmonised like angels. With Hughes at the helm, The Corrs threw themselves into becoming a proper band. They rehearsed in an improvised studio in a bedroom at Jim's, furnished with bits and pieces borrowed from the kitchen and acoustically engineered with empty egg cartons.

The Corrs' first ever amateur pop video has the four standing behind their microphone stands, the girls dressed in blue and white, *sans* instruments, and Jim in jacket and jeans on guitar. It didn't set any precedents, but it was a start. What they needed were some amateur gigs. Ironically, their first public performance took place at The Waterfront, the venue for the *Commitments* auditions. The place was jam-packed with friends, relations (including, naturally enough, Jean and Gerry) and a smattering of Hughes' showbiz mates, keen to see if the siblings matched up to the hype. Needless to say, they went down a storm.

The Corrs set about familiarising themselves with playing live. There was a special *Commitments* live concert, after which – with Hughes' encouragement and school homework permitting – the band began playing a myriad of venues around Dublin and Dundalk. They quickly built up a loyal local following, but there was still one thing missing: a drummer. Caroline decided to keep it in the family, and co-opted a boyfriend into teaching her to play. Now complete, The Corrs played and practised for three whole years before they felt ready to headline their first professional engagement, at Whelans Music Bar in Dublin. Dressed in black, a Celtic cross around Andrea's neck, and with their swirling Celtic insignia in place as a backdrop, they went down a storm and were met with whoops, cheers and thunderous applause. A sign, indeed, of things to come.

Dressed in black, a Celtic cross around Andrea's neck, and with their swirling Celtic insignia in place as a backdrop, they went down a storm

By a strange stroke of luck, at the back of the audience was Jean Kennedy Smith, the then American ambassador to Ireland. Invited to come along by Bill Whelan, the distinguished Kennedy Smith was bowled by over the stunning foursome. She extended an invitation for them to play at a VIP function at the Kennedy Library in Boston for her brother, Senator Ted Kennedy, and to play in front of the Taoiseach (Irish Prime Minister) at the soccer World Cup. John Hughes swiftly raised the money for their airfares. Though a record deal still eluded The Corrs, it was a situation their manager now felt confident of remedying.

Jim Corr

James Stephen Ignatius Corr says his best musical experience so far has been kicking off The Corrs' world tour to a 'mad, screaming audience' in Ireland. If he has any vices, they include killing a funny joke by retelling it once too often, and a bit of grumpiness when overtired. He likes people who focus on the positive, and doesn't like those who bitch about others because of their own insecurities. He wears contact lenses or glasses and a silver ring on his thumb, has a full driving license and simply wants to make people happy through his music. Blue-eyed Jim has described The Corrs as 'the greatest thing since sliced bread'.

Though adamant that The Corrs have no designated leader, and that all decisions are made both diplomatically and democratically, this eldest Corr is often considered the driving force behind the group's musical direction. It was Jim, after all, who was dreaming of family rock stardom while Andrea and Caroline were still poring over their schoolbooks at Dun Lughaidh Convent, and Sharon was slogging it out in various orchestras and managing a local record shop. As the most senior Corr by six years, Jim – who was born on 31 July 1964 – had the foresight to realise that the musical success and recognition he craved could be obtained from the people sitting around him at the Dundalk dinner table.

His earliest memories are musical ones. As a toddler, Jim would stand on tiptoe to bash the keys of the old piano in his bedroom, until Gerry recognised his potential and took him in hand with regular lessons. Thus began a lifelong passion for music – today he lists classical music among his interests, putting it down to Gerry's aptitude on both the organ and piano.

Dolores Keane

Jim quickly mastered the piano. He kept playing and practising as he grew up, eventually sharing the instrument with his equally zealous sisters. In adolescence he took up the keyboard and synthesiser, which – as a self-conscious youth – he thought to be considerably cooler than the rather stuffy piano.

In Dundalk, music is second nature. When the opportunity to learn another instrument presented itself, Jim seized it. His next-door neighbour taught him the guitar at an early age. Today it's the one thing Jim says he would take with him to a desert island (his chosen desert island disc, by the way, would be Fleetwood Mac's legendary *Rumours*). His passion for guitars embraces the archetypal rock star's electric Fender Stratocasters and Telecasters, as well as the acoustic, older-style brands such as Gretsch and Gibson, favoured by country and western singers.

A stint playing

with the

traditional singer

Dolores Keane

threw Jim in at

the deep end

Being preoccupied with his keyboards and guitar meant that the teenage Jim's school work suffered during his time at De La Salle Brothers Catholic school. While his sisters all received above-average grades, Jim Corr wasn't exactly a model student, as his school reports testify. Sharon has spoken of a time when the police came calling on the Corr home, wanting to speak to Jim. Apparently they had extinguished a bonfire that had been blazing dangerously close to a chemical plant. Jim, blissfully unaware of any risks, had got it going again. The nickname 'arsonist' stuck for a bit. He suspects it was Sharon who had grassed on him, but has added it was probably for good reason.

He had also fallen in with a bad crowd: a group of youths who would cruise the streets of Dundalk, looking for cars to steal. And while Jim was never involved in any of the thefts, he has admitted he got a thrill out of hanging out with those who were. He felt dangerous by association. Jim might have hung out with the wild bunch, but luckily his heart was in his music and he outgrew his thieving cronies. A fascination with all things electronic had made him pause and consider taking up electronics as a career, but he opted ultimately for music, briefly attending music college on leaving school.

By the age of 15 Jim had already begun performing with his parents in Dundalk's bars and clubs, joining in their repertoire of hits by the likes of The Eagles, Simon and Garfunkel, Abba and the Carpenters. Though happy to perform spot-on renditions of the music he'd grown up listening to, Jim was simultaneously developing his own musical tastes. He listened to albums by bands such as Horslips, Prefab Sprout, Scritti Politti and The Police. He has said the latter's 'Message In a Bottle' still sends shivers up his spine.

Although Jim was familiar with folk music, he had never actually learned how to play it. A televised concert by singer/songwriters Paul Brady and Andy Irvine impressed him enough to want to start. Brady and Irvine had both been members of Planxty, the internationally acclaimed group who in the 1970s revolutionised the way young Irish people felt about the old folk repertoire. After Planxty split up in 1975, Brady and Irvine continued to record together. Indeed, their 1976 album, *Andy Irvine and Paul Brady* is said to be one of the finest recordings of Irish music ever made. In tribute to the music which inspired Jim, The Corrs were happy to perform on Brady's 1995 album, *Spirits Colliding*.

A stint playing with the traditional singer Dolores Keane threw Jim in at the deep end, and he was soon in his element. Keane hails from Caherlistrane in County Galway, where her family has lived for five generations. She was raised on traditional music, and although she also plays rock, traditional is what she's known and loved best for.

De Dannen, Keane's original band, rivalled The Chieftains as an Irish institution. They were a group of virtuoso instrumentalists who incorporated fiddle, flute, bouzouki,

WHILE THE OTHERS ARE TUCKED UP IN BED AFTER
ANOTHER EXHAUSTING GIG, JIM CAN BE FOUND
CHECKING OUT THE NIGHTCLUBS OF THE WORLD

His guitar playing has been praised for its dexterity, innovation and phrasing

bodhrán, bones, banjo, viola, guitar and many other sounds into their wild and wonderful mix. This famed Galway band included everyone from Keane to Mary Black and Maura O'Connell in its line-up; it continues to carry on the tradition today. Keane, who left De Dannen in the mid-1970s to perform with her husband John Faulkner, has been called 'the voice of Ireland'. Who better, then, to teach Jim Corr the sounds he'd later combine with pop-rock to superb effect in The Corrs.

Jim enjoyed gigging with Keane during the 1980s – he even visited New Zealand with

her as part of a sponsored tour of Irish music – but eventually he was drawn to more chart-friendly music. He joined an electro-pop outfit called The Fountainhead, who were founded by Steve Belton and Pat O'Donnell, and whose debut single 'Rhythm Method' was a dancefloor hit. But despite an international deal, The Fountainhead were unable to deliver the goods in the long term. Sales from their two albums were poor and they were dropped from their record company. Jim formed his own band, Chip, hoping for great things, but received knockbacks instead. He began playing with a band called Hinterland, which featured Gerry Leonard on guitar and Donal Coughlan on vocals/guitar. Their debut album, *Kissing the Roof of Heaven* made little impact on the charts, and in time they too split up.

Jim continued to work regularly as a session musician, but he was becoming increasingly frustrated. Nevertheless, he's said that these knockbacks enabled him to cope with the refusals The Corrs received in their early days. To pay the bills, he and Sharon had also started gigging as a traditional duo, playing and singing old ballads. He had an inkling, however, that he only need look to his own backyard for collaborators. The makeshift studio in the house he rented was being increasingly frequented by his sisters.

By the time Andrea was 15, all the Corr children would come together to create songs. Jim would develop ideas and melody lines, and the girls came up with the words. As they all became united in their desire to make it as a band, Jim and his three sisters began to rehearse as often as homework permitted. At the weekends they would often play until three or four in the morning to get their songs just right. So when a friend tipped him off about the *Commitments* auditions being held at The Waterfront, Jim thought that The Corrs could be in with a chance – and he was right.

Jim is only too happy to acknowledge the inroads made by the Irish bands who have gone before The Corrs. The success of U2 and the Cranberries persuaded record companies to give more time to Irish artists; The Corrs are surfing in their wake. One of the more ambitious Corrs, Jim feels strongly that hard work and record sales should be celebrated, and happily accepts any of the numerous awards that come his way. And as far as adulation from fans goes, his sisters jokingly maintain that Jim gets more attention than all of them put together. Jim, on the other hand, jokes that he is only there to make the girls look good. He has said that he is often literally pushed to one side by fans eager to get to Andrea, Caroline and Sharon, a state of affairs he is quite happy about. Being forever in the shadow of his sisters means he gets to have more fun.

Jim Corr is The Corrs' resident party animal. While the others are tucked up in bed after another exhausting gig, Jim can be found checking out the nightclubs of the world.

In Singapore, for example, he was seen at Club Zouk; in Australia he frequented the late night watering holes on Queensland's Hamilton Island. In Halifax, Canada, he was spotted with his sisters at an open mike club called Birdland, unsuccessfully attempting to get the girls onstage with him to do an incognito turn as the 'Corr Blimeys'. 'We do go mad from time to time,' he told *Sky* magazine, 'but when we get into our hotel rooms, we generally just go to sleep in our beds. We're so tired. We're not really up to throwing television sets out of windows.' Still, he did find time to go bungee jumping last time he was in Australia, an experience he found both terrifying and exhilarating.

Live, Jim's guitar manner is as laid-back as his personality, and he makes playing complicated pieces on the keyboards look deceptively easy, even with his guitar still slung around his neck. His guitar playing has been praised for its dexterity, innovation

Jim firmly believes in dressing up and looking good when performing

and phrasing. Where his sisters' stage presence is serene and elegant, Jim grins delightedly into any TV cameras which may be present – the mark of a man thoroughly enjoying himself. Although he has got used to playing to 10,000 people one day and 300 the next, Jim still has bouts of missing Dundalk – specifically, his friends, parents, car and the Dundalk-brewed McCardles Brown Ale. He loves Ireland, especially the stretch along the west coast from Donegal to Killarney. With a bit of nudging, he says he might consider settling in Stockholm or certain parts of Australia one day, but that Dundalk would always be considered home. Because The Corrs devote so much time to signing autographs and chatting to fans after their shows, and rarely get any time off, Jim politely requests that they give him some privacy when he's back at the Dundalk family home.

All this touring means he hasn't got around to buying a place of his own yet. It has also taken its toll on his love life: Jim is, apparently, 'still looking'. He has said that his sisters would never directly tell him if they didn't like someone he was dating, but would, of course, talk behind his back instead.

Those that reckon Jim is the luckiest man in the world forget that Sharon, Caroline and Andrea are actually his kid sisters. They are the girls with whom he's battled to get into the bathroom for years (the reason, perhaps, behind the fact that Jim is always the

This affable

and easy-going

big brother is

usually the

quietest Corr

during press

interviews

last to surface for breakfast when they're on the road). They are the very same sisters he might have bossed around when they were tiny, but no longer. As he's said, no-one tells Irish girls what to do. He reckons that their most annoying habit is making him wait while they all get ready – just like being married three times over!

This affable and easy-going big brother is usually the quietest Corr during press interviews, taking the ribbing his sisters routinely give him about stealing their lingerie or borrowing their lipstick with a bemused smile. While this is unlikely to say the least, with his leather trousers, quiff and closely razored sideburns (a look some have likened to Jason Priestly's Brandon in *Beverly Hills 90210*) Jim firmly believes in dressing up and looking good when performing.

Something that Jim is seriously unamused about is bootlegging, both of The Corrs' recordings and of music in general. Piracy, he feels, harms the record industry by taking money out of the pockets of songwriters and musicians. He'd sign almost anything for a fan, as he acknowledges that the fans are The Corrs' livelihood (he's just bought a laptop computer so he can check out the wealth of Corrs websites). Just don't ask him to autograph a pirate copy of a Corrs gig.

If, as with the Fleetwood Mac *Legacy* album, there was ever a tribute album to The Corrs, Jim would be honoured if Natalie Imbruglia, Sting and Jewel would contribute to it. If he ever has children, he'd like them to do jobs that utilised their talents; the most enjoyment you can get out of your work, he believes, is when you're doing a job that is your hobby as well.

Jim comes across as rather a deep thinker in interviews, and is not averse to a spot of philosophising, asking big questions like 'Why are we here?' He's concluded that life is all about learning, and compassion – a philosophy which he often hints at in his lyrics. The Corrs' success, he feels, is an excellent example of mind over matter. That is, if you want something bad enough, think about it constantly and make positive moves to get it, you can achieve anything.

Getting the deal

In the summer of 1994, four excited Corrs boarded a plane bound for Boston, ostensibly for the *craic*, but with each of them harbouring a desire to land a hefty recording contract. There had been publishing deals back home, and offers which sounded promising but had failed to come to fruition. Given John Hughes' contacts, they could probably have signed to an Irish major. But they collectively decided to hold out for a deal which would not only give them enough independence to make their own decisions, but would also have the financial muscle to introduce The Corrs to the world. What The Corrs needed to hit the big time was to sign to a big American label.

Their polished performances in Boston wowed the city and turned Senator Ted Kennedy into an ardent fan overnight. (He later bought a block of one hundred tickets to The Corrs' 1996 tour with Celine Dion.) Encouraged, Hughes took his protégés to labels in New York and Los Angeles, anticipating that they too would be bowled over. Nothing happened. The fact that their music eschewed categorisation counted against them in a highly competitive market where categories and labels are all important.

Undeterred, John Hughes and The Corrs headed back to New York, where they turned up unannounced at Atlantic Records and asked to see Jason Lom, head of A&R (Artists and Repertoire). At Hughes' invitation, Lom was among the pogoing crowd at the Whelans gig in Dublin, where The Corrs played tracks like 'Love to Love You' and

'Someday' alongside traditional numbers such as 'Toss the Feathers' and 'The Carraroe Jig'. And when all four Corrs strutted into his office looking stunning and touting a demo tape full of potential hit singles, an overawed Lom thought they were just what his new company, Lava (a subsidiary of Atlantic), needed. He suggested they meet with the man who joined Atlantic Records as Vice President in 1994, the 14-time Grammy Award-winning producer David Foster.

Foster, however, was ensconced over at the Hit Factory in Manhattan, working with Michael Jackson on his *HIStory* album. Jackson and his then wife Lisa Marie Presley had come hoping that Foster would work his Midas touch and kickstart Jackson's somewhat stalled career. Consequently, The Corrs couldn't get an appointment. But because they were flying home the following day and had nothing to lose except their pride, they

WHAT THE CORRS NEEDED TO HIT THE BIG TIME WAS TO SIGN TO A BIG AMERICAN LABEL

decided to take matters into their own fair hands. Dressed in their stage finery, they took a deep breath and, armed with their instruments, marched down a blazing hot Eighth Avenue and into the Hit Factory reception. They looked so dramatic that it's likely the staff thought they were meant to be there.

Nevertheless, Jackson's ever-vigilant security made it impossible to get to Foster. They sat themselves down on a plush sofa and waited. And waited. But as it turned out, and as luck would have it, Foster was just winding up his work on *HIStory*. At the end of a long day, when he finally emerged, tired and ready to put his feet up, he was greeted with a vision of loveliness (and their reasonably handsome brother). On hearing that The Corrs were heading back to Ireland the next morning and simply wanted the chance to play for him, Foster found it impossible to say no. He ushered them into a small studio. There, with Jim on the piano and his sisters gathered around with bodhrán (Foster admits that back then he didn't even know what a bodhrán was), whistle and violin, they sang a few acoustic numbers and their now familiar hits, 'Runaway' and 'Forgiven, Not Forgotten'. Foster was hooked. He later commented that he knew he was witnessing real talent – on a scale of one to ten, he gave them a ten plus. He wanted to sign them up

immediately, as the first act on his new Atlantic label, 143.

The Corrs have said they didn't realise how much of Foster's music they had already listened to and loved at the time of their meeting. Foster has worked with a galaxy of mainstream superstars in a career which spans nearly 30 years. Little known to those outside the music industry, he is referred to within the biz as the 'King of Pop', reflecting his chart-busting work with the likes of Whitney Houston, Celine Dion, Michael Bolton, En Vogue and Kenny G. Between 1994 and 1997 he held the number one spot on the Billboard Hot 100 for twenty per cent of the time. Not since the legendary producer George Martin (of Beatles fame) has one man led the charts for so long. Unsurprising, then, that The Corrs gatecrashed The Hit Factory to meet him.

The eventual deal with Foster was worth a rumoured UK£750,000 ($1m), which the forward-thinking Corrs immediately ploughed back into recording and touring.

Of course there have been low points: a San Diego radio station once got them to sing *a capella* to a listener while they were standing in the pouring rain. And at the end of a demanding few months of international dates, they came down with a collective dose of flu as they were about to play Dublin's most prestigious venue, The Point. Sharon, who'd had a high fever, dragged herself out of bed to play. The overjoyed audience was none the wiser.

The Corrs realised early on that the only way to international stardom, the only way to get their music to a large number of people, was through sheer hard work. John Hughes has often likened their rise to fame to the ascent of a difficult and steep mountain face. With Hughes in tow, they embarked on a gruelling two-and-a-half-year world tour, collecting fans by the million in the process. No promotional opportunity was turned down, no interview spurned. For a couple of hours after each concert they made themselves available to sign autographs and to pose for pictures. As a result of this effort, *Forgiven, Not Forgotten* went gold and platinum in ten countries, and number one records ensued, from Norway to New Zealand (although chart recognition still eluded them in the UK and America).

'I think a big secret to our success so far is the fact that we communicate and get on very well with people,' Sharon told Ireland's *Hot Press*. 'We're willing to do as much as is required of us. We're willing to put in all the effort and we do make a serious effort to get

on with everybody we're working with and do as much as we can. And if you work hard
enough and people see that you're working hard and that they can get on with you, then
they've a tendency to work with you rather than work against you. So that, to my mind, is
what it's all about. It's about communication.'

Believe it or not, one of their more nerve-wracking moments in 1996 was returning
home to perform in Dundalk and Dublin. Playing in front of the people they grew up with
was the trickiest test of all, especially with an audience that included ex-music teachers,
next-door neighbours, old school mates and cast-off boyfriends and girlfriends. Naturally
enough, they went down a storm.

In Dublin they were to play before a crowd of 25,000 at the Landsdowne Road
stadium, the highlight of their career to date. Though looking the picture of confidence in

Offscreen, they

bonded with

Jason Priestly,

who brought

them a few

Canadian beers

a slinky black slip and Dr Marten's boots, Andrea was so nervous before the show that she couldn't speak. But fuelled by an up-for-it crowd who held banners emblazoned with the words 'Dublin Loves The Corrs', the band couldn't put a foot wrong. Ecstatic, they dedicated a song to Jean Kennedy Smith ('A special friend of ours in the audience'), the woman they credit with giving them their first start.

There have been plenty of memorable live appearances back home since then. For example, they provided the opening entertainment in Dublin's Croke Park for an internationally televised NFL game between American football stars the Chicago Bears and the Pittsburgh Steelers, performing 'The Star Spangled Banner'.

The band followed up *Forgiven, Not Forgotten* with 1997's *Talk On Corners*, which was produced partly by Jim, and with Foster retaining a hand in the overall sound. After another hugely successful world tour, The UK was still slow to pick up on the charms of the sibling quartet. But it was about to have the Corr experience beamed directly into its living room. On the evening of St Patrick's Day, 1998, the BBC broadcast The Corrs live in concert at the Royal Albert Hall. Almost overnight, Britain was won over. All The Corrs had needed, it seemed, was to be seen *and* heard.

The band have an uncanny knack for being in the right place at the right time. For example, in 1996, John Hughes and David Foster were eating in a Los Angeles restaurant. Aaron Spelling, a friend of Foster's and executive producer of *Dallas*, *Dynasty* and the hugely popular American TV series *Beverly Hills 90210*, happened to be dining at the next table. Hughes was introduced to Spelling, who revealed that *The Commitments* was one of his favourite films. Hughes then began waxing lyrical about his fabulous charges, The Corrs. Spelling offered to audition them for *90210*, and, like everyone else, was astounded at their combination of beauty and musical prowess. He offered them a slot on the hit show. The Corrs flew into Los Angeles during a break as support on Celine Dion's European tour to appear on a *Beverly Hills 90210* New Year's Eve special.

They performed 'Forgiven, Not Forgotten' in the fictional local club called the Peach Pit. The dulcet strains of 'Runaway' featured as background music during some of the episode's more poignant scenes, and one of the series' characters name-checked The Corrs in the script. Offscreen, they bonded with Jason Priestly, who brought them a few Canadian beers – although at seven in the morning they thought it was a little early to open them. All agree that appearing on the show was great exposure.

Still, as humble as ever, they say felt a bit like impostors who shouldn't be there: four

kids from Dundalk in the middle of LA! Needless to say, they looked perfectly at home in their new surroundings. After filming from 7am through to 8pm, they hopped on a plane to New York and went straight onto a morning chat show, then flew back to Los Angeles for a *Billboard* convention.

The Corrs have become adept at television appearances, and are in demand from TV shows around the world. Some of their more notable special guest slots have included *Kelly Live* in Ireland; *The Jose Carreras Gala* in Germany; *Good Morning with Richard and*

Judy, *Surprise Surprise* and the *National Lottery Live* (where they played alongside Rod Stewart) in Great Britain. In the US they have appeared on *Today*, *CBS This Morning*, *Late Night with Conan O'Brien*, *Letterman* and the aforementioned *Beverly Hills 90210*. They have also made several appearances on the chart show they grew up watching: *Top of the Pops*.

After feeling slightly out of place alongside Jason Priestly and his co-stars, The Corrs are now getting used to mixing with people they'd only ever watched on TV and in the movies. They've discussed vegetarianism with Warren Beatty and his wife Annette Bening, and shared a drink or two with Sean Penn. They have been at parties with Kevin Costner (Caroline didn't realise who he was when she shook hands with him) and David Hasselhoff from *Baywatch*.

But their brushes with the stars didn't end there. Andrea went from *The Commitments* to acting alongside Madonna and Jonathan Pryce in Alan Parker's *Evita*.

The Corrs are now getting used to mixing with people they'd only ever watched on TV and in the movies

They've met Hilary Clinton, duetted with Pavarotti, supported the Rolling Stones and shared the stage with the likes of Stevie Wonder and the Spice Girls. But the figure who inspired the most awe was the person these Catholic boys and girls had grown up revering: the Pope.

The Corrs were each granted a private audience with the Pontiff in December 1997, during a break in rehearsals for an all-star Vatican Christmas show. The line-up included blues guitarist BB King, soul singer Chaka Kahn and a plethora of French and Italian opera stars. The Corrs, who sang *Silent Night* with the backing of a 100-piece orchestra, have said that their real rehearsal for the meeting in Rome's holy city had begun ten years beforehand, when they would gather around the piano to sing Christmas carols. Prior to meeting the Pope in his rooms, the group sat together in total silence. John Hughes led them in individually, later revealing that the Pontiff smiled on being told they were Irish, presented each with a set of rosary beads he had blessed and wished them a Happy Christmas. It was a great end to what had been a great year.

SHARON CORR

Green-eyed Sharon Corr was born on 23 March, 1970. Diplomatic as well as beautiful, she is reluctant to list her most memorable musical experience so far, preferring to say that playing live anywhere is always wonderful. She has observed that one of the nicest things about fame is meeting interesting people, and receiving little gifts – such as the smelling salts in a silver container she received from a Singapore fan. Sharon's sunny nature is complemented by the fact she is eternally optimistic, a woman who prefers to look on the bright side of any dilemma. It's this attitude which has helped The Corrs through the darker days when they were initially turned down by American labels as being too folk for pop, or too pop for folk. As the composed and capable eldest sister, Sharon felt quietly confident that The Corrs' persistence would pay dividends. She was right.

Sharon has a soft spot for honest people. She dislikes anyone who seems insincere, or who chatters on merely for the sake of hearing their own voice. She doesn't have a driving licence, was once a vegetarian, and admits that the one thing she could never do without is coffee. Keen to keep things as honest and real as possible, she has admitted that one of her faults is a tendency towards dogmatism.

Jim, Andrea and Caroline have unanimously (and fondly) elected her the bossiest Corr, although Sharon would prefer to call herself organised rather than bossy. While the others are faffing around in some international airport terminal, it is Sharon who keeps hold of all the tickets and passports, who makes sure that everyone is ready to leave on time, and that they have packed suitable clothing for sun, snow, or whatever climate they

Sharon's teacher wasted no time in drawing out her potential, and instilled in her the love of classical music she has today

might be heading off to. Jim likes to tease his sister about her spending, particularly the size of her mobile phone bill, which he says is by far the largest of all of them. Sharon, however, will always point out that she is as organised in her finances as she is with the rest of her life.

Born six years after Jim, Sharon started playing the piano as soon as she could reach the keys. As much as Jim loved the instrument, and despite the fact that it was situated in *his* bedroom, he was unable to claim a monopoly over his three younger sisters.

Sharon started to learn the violin at the age of six. The story goes that Gerry and Jean Corr had heard about a new method of violin teaching which was particularly suitable for very young children. But it wasn't the piano-playing Sharon they had in mind at all; it was her little sister Caroline, who was three at the time. It's probably safe to say that two-year-old Andrea was only just getting around to bashing the odd piano key! The Corrs Senior invited their local priest Father McNally, a musical man who knew a thing or two about violins, to instruct their second youngest in the art of string instruments. But Caroline was so terrified by this large man in black that Gerry and Jean were forced to rethink their strategy.

They decided to make a trip to another classical violin teacher in Dundalk, in the hope that Caroline would be too distracted by her new surroundings to be frightened. She was distracted alright – Corr family lore has it that this time Caroline was so fascinated with the size of the violin teacher's ears and his bald, shiny head that any plans to transform her into a tiny violin-playing protegy flew out the window. Jean and Gerry decided that Sharon should be taught how to play the child-size instrument instead.

Sharon's teacher wasted no time in drawing out her potential, and instilled in her the love of classical music she has today. As Sharon grew, so did her violin, and a larger model was bought every other year. This violin teacher knew promise when he saw it (he often sent his charges on to music conservatoires in Berkeley and Vienna) and with his encouragement Sharon practised daily. Between the ages of 7 and 14 she was a member of the Redeemer Youth Orchestra, a body of young musicians who played together on stringed, wind and percussion instruments. Founded and voluntarily run by Father McNally, Sharon and the rest of the orchestra would practise for three hours every Friday evening. Sharon played second violin, part of a support section to the first violinists (who got to play all the best tunes).

Founded by Father McNally in the mid-1970s, the Redeemer Youth Orchestra became renowned in County Louth for its fine musicianship. Comprised entirely of volunteers, it has performed regularly in concerts and competitions, with various individual members

She is hard-working and ambitious, quick witted and funny, sexy and sophisticated, caring and confident

competing in the country's numerous All Ireland Championships. As its reputation spread, so did the demand: the orchestra toured the East Coast of America in the early 1980s. At least ten graduates of the Redeemer Youth Orchestra now play in top Irish and European orchestras.

The orchestra played pieces by some of the composers Sharon cites as her favourites today, including Tchaikovsky, Britten, and Dvořák. Sharon has also said she admires the work of Frenchman Eric Satie. Sharon also has a genuine love for heavy rock music, and counts The Rolling Stones as one of her all-time favourite acts. She had been shaking her head along to the Stones' distinctive guitar riffs and vocal gymnastics since she was a teenager, but The Corrs' three support gigs to the Stones (in Prague, Mannheim and Berlin) have cemented what was already a life-long admiration. Sharon has said she definitely doesn't want to be touring with The Corrs when she's 60. But the energy emanating from the stage at those gigs confirmed her belief that the Rolling Stones have

As a teenager, Sharon papered her bedroom with posters of British soul singer Paul Young

that indefinable something which puts them a league above the rest. Jagger, she feels, was born to rock 'n' roll. It's a compliment he returned by dancing at the side of the stage during The Corrs' red hot sets – something he allegedly hasn't done since the Stones played with Bob Dylan way back in the 1960s.

Sharon Corr wasn't exactly a model student of the Dun Lughaidh Convent: she was suspended from school twice. Both times were for what the Irish call 'mitching' and the English call 'bunking off', that is, she skipped lessons. She only did it twice, and was caught both times. Sharon maintains that she rarely did anything wrong, but when she tried to rebel she was always caught out. Today her most rebellious habit is smoking; she says that all four Corrs work so hard and tour so much that leading a drink 'n' drugs lifestyle would result in collective collapse.

On the other hand, Sharon doesn't see that being in a band with her siblings puts any restrictions on her lifestyle. 'If you can't stand on your own and decide what you want to do, then you're a bit sad,' she said in *Sky* magazine. 'If I was of the personality that wanted to go round spitting and drinking copious amounts of alcohol and doing lots of drugs then I'd be doing it...' Luckily for them, she isn't that sort of person.

As a teenager, Sharon papered her bedroom with posters of British soul singer Paul Young, a typical schoolgirl crush which she still cringes about today. The Corrs actually met Young recently on a TV show; Jim has joked that he was tempted to tell the singer about Sharon's former infatuation. That isn't to say that Sharon didn't have any boyfriends of her own, of course, and indeed both Andrea and Caroline had crushes on a couple of them. Today she enjoys the most long-term relationship of all the band, with a tall, fair-haired Belfast barrister named Gavin Bonner.

Sharon met Gavin over three years ago, on the day The Corrs were shooting their first video, 'Runaway'. They've been together ever since, in spite of the long separations necessitated by Sharon's demanding touring schedule. She moved to Belfast to live with him in October 1998. The couple have a four-bedroomed house in the upmarket Stranmillis area, where Sharon has been seen around town in jeans and a T-shirt,

ONSTAGE, SHARON HAS A SERENE, ELEGANT PRESENCE

stocking up on groceries at the local Sainsburys. She has said she is optimistic that the still-fragile peace agreements will eventually put an end to the Troubles, and rates the inhabitants of Belfast as some of the nicest, most welcoming people she's ever encountered.

With all the success The Corrs have achieved, Sharon craves a bit of normality, if only to keep her feet on the ground. If she's able to get home during a few days' break in touring, she tends to get stuck into giving the house a top-to-toe spring clean. She also likes to get back to her local pub in Dundalk, where she can relax with a drink and old friends. Sharon found Los Angeles, where The Corrs recorded *Talk on Corners*, a stark contrast to her home. For starters, to buy anything you had to drive for miles, whereas in Dundalk you could just pop out to the local shop. In LA Sharon found herself being told the life stories of waiters and waitresses within minutes, in the hope that she could help them to further their acting careers.

Sharon is philosophical about the obstacles international superstardom poses for her love life. For one thing, being apart so much means you never take the other person for granted. Although it often feels like you're starting all over again after a break of two months, it also invests the relationship with a freshness and renewed excitement. Sharon has said she feels lucky to have found a partner with a strong sense of self, someone who understands the pressures of the music industry and is prepared to get on with his own life while she is away.

Sharon went on to play in a variety of other orchestras after leaving the Redeemer Youth Orchestra. After leaving Dun Lughaigh Convent she worked in a Dundalk record shop, a job in which she was surrounded by music she loved and which introduced her to a wide variety of new artists. She and Jim, who was struggling to make ends meet as a rock musician, formed a traditional duo and played in some of Dundalk's bars and clubs. Then came those auditions for *The Commitments*, and the rest, as they say, is history.

The Corrs' eldest sister has attributed much of the band's success to the understanding, encouragement and musical know-how of their parents, Jean and Gerry. She has admitted that she and her sisters used to fight as kids, but they have all matured since The Corrs hit the charts, and rarely do so now. Sibling rivalry rarely, if ever, occurs, but they've said that when it does it's usually during a photo shoot, when one of them is feeling inadequate or ugly.

Onstage, Sharon has a serene, elegant presence. It's bolstered by the black electric violin she holds down by her side when singing backing vocals, or cradles under her chin to wring out its soaring, soothing notes. She is often asked why The Corrs don't incorporate more violin solos into their music in order to display this virtuosity. The answer is that they do so when they can, but that not all The Corrs songs lend themselves to this approach.

Sharon is always perfectly groomed for live shows, favouring long, beautifully cut black coats, black trousers and high heels. She doesn't usually wear nail polish, but her make-up often consists of gold or green eyeshadow which has been smudged for extra effect. She loves doing photo shoots, being dressed up and having her face done, even though she thinks it is all a bit bizarre. Her strong, sweet vocals provide the perfect back-up to Andrea's clarion-like lead, but where Andrea is all grand, theatrical gestures, Sharon's demeanour is more understated. Nevertheless, her love of the music is palpable: she'll often mouth Andrea's words, dance gracefully on the spot, or flash a radiant smile to the crowd.

Like all her siblings, Sharon takes a while to come back down after a gig. She'll often lead the others in a deconstruction of the evening, pointing out its high and low points and concentrating on areas which need working on. Because anyone would get a bit tired of playing the same songs repeatedly, Sharon lists her favourite Corrs song as the most recent addition to the set, or the most recent one they've written. She feels that the best way to perfect one's craft is to be thrown in at the deep end, and has cited The Corrs' first television appearance alongside a 100-piece orchestra as an example.

Sharon and the rest of The Corrs are happy to take advantage of any promotional opportunity; sometimes, however, they should check the weather report first. She happened to be wearing a short pink dress during The Corrs' visit to the *JFK* aircraft carrier in Dublin Bay, and the blustery wind gave hordes of sailors ample photo opportunity to glimpse Sharon's behind as she climbed back down a ladder to the docks!

Sharon Corr is said to possess a combination of the positive characteristics of her brother and sisters. She is hard-working and ambitious, quick witted and funny, sexy and

The Corrs'
eldest sister has
attributed much
of the band's
success to the
understanding,
encouragement
and musical
know-how of
their parents

sophisticated, caring and confident. Jim often seeks her advice on relationships; Andrea and Caroline also look up to their older sister for counsel. Sharon puts her demeanour down to being Irish. Her countryfolk, she has said, are blessed with a lot of hope and an ability to thoroughly enjoy themselves. There's also a mystical, haunting quality to the land that influences how she feels and what she plays.

Inspirations

The Chieftains

As perhaps the most prominent and accessible ambassadors for Irish traditional music around the world, The Corrs have always acknowledged the debt they owe to the folk musicians who inspired them. But they are just part of the growing movement to incorporate the sounds of traditional Irish music into mainstream pop.

At one time the concept of an Irish 'sound' was thought only to cover more tradition-based acts such as The Dubliners, The Fureys, De Dannen and the venerable Chieftains, but today it has broadened to incorporate a whole spectrum of musical genres. From Clannad and Enya to Boyzone and B*Witched, Irish musicians have been referring to their Celtic roots in their lyrics, musical forms and rhythms, creating a distinct Irish sound in the process. Growing up hearing the traditional music of their ancestors played by their parents and others, while enjoying a healthy interest in pop, it seems only natural for The Corrs to mix the two together.

Those attending The Corrs' concerts for the first time often expect little more than some pleasant entertainment from a vocal group, and are consequently astounded at the band's instrumental skills. With Caroline on bodhrán, Andrea on tin whistle and Sharon playing a blend of classical and traditional compositions on the violin, their music is a seamless mixture of the traditional and the modern; an 'updating' of tunes and rhythms which have evolved over hundreds of years of Irish history.

It is really only in the last 15 years or so that non-Irish listeners have become used to hearing Irish folk music regularly. Certainly the recent worldwide phenomenon of *Riverdance*, a touring stage show which mixed Irish music with non-stop traditional dancing, opened audiences' ears to the passion and beauty inherent in Irish culture. The

nation's love of self-expression is conveyed in music that demands active involvement from the listener.

Because Irish traditional music has been handed down through generations by word of mouth, without being written down, it has avoided being misrepresented in the way folk music has in some European countries. What we hear in Ireland today is what was played in the 18th and 19th centuries, although it has, admittedly, come about rather circuitously. When the widespread Irish famine of the mid-19th century forced much of the population to seek out a better life in the United States of America, individuals and families departed by boat, leaving their possessions behind. They took little with them apart from the songs and melodies they had committed to memory. On arrival, they dispersed across America, and their music travelled with them.

The major catalyst for the dissemination of Irish traditional music, both nationally and around the world, was the invention of the record. After the folk tunes were committed to disc, the recordings were sent back home to the 32 counties of the Emerald Isle. Things turned full circle. Most of the popular music – before and after the migrations – was dance music. Played in kitchens and barns, at crossroads, weddings, wakes and celebrations, this rustic music's lively beat spoke from the heart of the Irish people, and became *the* favoured form of entertainment.

Because the tradition is essentially an unwritten one, individual musicians embellish and decorate these tunes with their own flourishes and quirks. The majority of tunes are played in 'sessions', where groups of people gather to drink, chat and play music. The Corrs have a great deal of respect for Dundalk's traditional players, and name Gerry O'Connor and Eithne Ni Uallachain as two of the more awe-inspiring locals. Sharon is particularly influenced by the soulful, measured violin playing of County Clare's famed Martin Hayes.

Two of the most popular forms of music for dancing are jigs and reels – a jig is a lively dance with a characteristic rhythm, usually played in compound duple or triple time; a reel a rapid, smoothly flowing dance for two or more couples, usually played in simple quadruple time. Then, among others, there are hornpipes (a solo dance in simple duple time), polkas (a round dance in quick duple time), and the melodious, often melancholy compositions called slow airs.

There are a lot of traditional pieces: in 1985 a country-wide survey put the number of jigs, reels and hornpipes in the national repertoire at over 6,000. Taking into account the

Played in kitchens and barns, at crossroads, weddings, wakes and celebrations, this rustic music's lively beat spoke from the heart of the Irish people

Clannad

Perhaps because of the respect with which they treat their ancestors' music, The Corrs have never had any complaints from purists about their renditions

fact that musicians are constantly adding to and changing their repertoire, today's figure would be considerably larger. There are two main types of traditional song: the haunting *sean nós*, usually sung in Gaelic, either unaccompanied or backed by a bodhrán; and the more familiar storytelling ballads. Strains of *sean nós* can be heard in singers from Sinead O'Connor to Enya and Mary Black.

Dancing isn't a prerequisite when listening to a dance tune, although as thousands of The Corrs' fans will testify, once the music starts it becomes nigh on impossible to sit still. After The Corrs had become a proper band they decided to include some old Irish numbers in their stage sets, adding their own arrangements, chords and riffs. These include the forceful 'Joy of Life', an instrumental led by Sharon on the fiddle. With Andrea playing dextrous tin whistle flurries or dancing wildly in circles, Caroline down the front on bodhrán before hotfooting it back to her drum kit, and Jim's fingers flying on the keyboards, this fast and furious number epitomises The Corrs' effortless *joie de vivre*. Somewhat confusingly, Irish tunes can have different titles: Jim has explained that 'Joy of Life' is the name of the first tune in the instrumental called 'Carraroe Jig' on *Forgiven, Not Forgotten*.

Other traditional instrumentals from The Corrs – which include modern loops and programming – include 'Erin Shore', which both opens and closes their debut album. There's 'The Minstrel Boy', 'Along With the Girls', and, on *Talk on Corners*, the Jim Corr-produced 'Paddy McCarthy'. None of The Corrs know who McCarthy was, nor, indeed, where the titles of any these songs originated from. But then neither do most people, although some maintain that 'Haste to the Wedding' was written by a couple of Donegal fiddlers.

'Toss the Feathers', a track on *Forgiven, Not Forgotten*, required a special rhythm section. The Corrs co-opted the talents of Neil Staubenhaus on bass and Simon Philips on drums; Caroline remembers marvelling at the sheer size of Philips' drum kit. She has since learned to play the part for live shows.

Although it doesn't appear on either album, the two-part instrumental, 'Haste to the Wedding', is another highlight of their live shows. Part One sees Sharon coaxing soaring, languorous notes from the violin nestled under her chin, closing her eyes as the music conjures visions of peat fires and mists over spray-tossed headlands. A swift segue into a foot-stomping, frenetic Part Two has audiences up and clapping along immediately; Andrea playing tin whistle and weaving her body along to the rhythm, Caroline down the front for an impassioned bodhrán solo before Jim joins in on guitar. Often, backing musician Conor Brady will deliver a solo spot on electric guitar – for The Corrs' Royal Albert Hall gig they were joined on drums by Mick Fleetwood.

Perhaps because of the respect with which they treat their ancestors' music, The Corrs have never had any complaints from purists about their renditions – quite the opposite, in fact. Working with Paddy Moloney and The Chieftains on a Celtic version of Jimi Hendrix's 'Little Wing' was seen as a tacit sign of approval from Ireland's old guard. Treated with uillean pipes, harp, flute and The Corrs' signature instruments, the electric guitar maestro's ode to freedom is transformed into an exercise in Celtic magic.

Founded in 1963, The Chieftains are arguably Ireland's premier musical ambassadors, a group of traditional musicians who got together with the general aim of preserving Ireland's cultural heritage

The Chieftains

Clannad

Founded in 1963, The Chieftains are arguably Ireland's premier musical ambassadors, a group of traditional musicians who got together with the general aim of preserving Ireland's cultural heritage. Impressed by the talented Corrs, main man Paddy Moloney rang John Hughes to invite the quartet to guest on a track called 'I Know My Love', on The Chieftains album *Tears of Stone*, released in February 1999. Collaborators on other tracks include such luminaries as Joni Mitchell, Sinead O'Connor and Mary Chapin Carpenter. In a classic example of managerial skill, Hughes suggested to his charges that they should ask The Chieftains to collaborate on 'Little Wing'. Paddy Moloney and crew happily agreed. And when the time came to record, they all just sat down together and played.

The Corrs readily acknowledge the doors opened for them by other Irish artists. In the 1960s, singer/songwriters such as Van Morrison and Rory Gallagher were synonymous with Irish music, 'Van the Man' going on to achieve iconic status. The 1970s saw hard rockers Thin Lizzy, folk rockers Horslips (who have directly influenced The Corrs), singer/songwriter Elvis Costello and punk-pop rebels the Boomtown Rats burst onto the world scene, while a band called U2 began planting the seeds for worldwide domination. U2 became one of Ireland's major exports, and have invested much of their earnings into

The Corrs

readily

acknowledge

the doors

opened for

them by other

Irish artists

creating a strong musical infrastructure back home in Dublin. The Corrs often rehearse at The Factory, a big Dublin warehouse space owned by U2.

In the 1980s, artists such as The Pogues, Sinead O'Connor, Hothouse Flowers, Enya and Christy Moore garnered universal acclaim. County Kildare-born Moore is often credited as the godfather of the current boom in Irish music. A fiery protest singer, guitarist and bodhrán player, Moore had been lead singer of Planxty. Moore went on to fuse traditional and rock with Moving Hearts, whose precedent-setting 1985 album *The Storm* transformed traditional viewpoints, and gave Moore his nickname, 'The Storm in a T-shirt'.

Nineties bands like The Cranberries, Ash, Boyzone, B*Witched and, of course, The Corrs, are making the world sit up and take notice. In a country without musical restrictions, these bands now constitute the Irish sound as much as elder statesmen like The Chieftains and The Dubliners. 'When you think of what U2 have done in terms of paving the way for an awful lot of bands, then you can really only be grateful to them,' Jim told *Hot Press*. 'I mean, I think that record companies now give new (Irish) bands the benefit of the doubt more often, certainly when it comes to checking them out or whatever.' Caroline continued that, 'People are all so different anyway. Like if you look at Ash, U2, The Cranberries – they're all miles apart. Everybody's miles apart as far as we're concerned. The way we see it, everybody's focus is different.'

In terms of increasing their profile in America, the band have nevertheless taken a leaf out of The Cranberries' book. The Cranberries did it the tough way, supporting bands and doing small headline spots. Before they knew it, they were selling hundreds of thousands of albums. Other outfits such as Altan and Clannad have continued to demonstrate that you can stay in the tradition and appeal to a modern audience. Altan, led by fiddler Mairead Ni Mhaonaigh and flautist Frankie Kennedy, maintain a traditional core repertoire with an emphasis on less-well-known material, but add the occasional rock flourish.

The Corrs cite Clannad (Gaelic for 'family'), a veritable music dynasty, as a major influence. Formed in 1980, the group was then comprised of family members Mary and Enya Brennan, brothers Paul and Ciaran and uncles Padraig and Noel Duggan. With celestial vocals originally sung in Gaelic, backed by harp, flute, acoustic guitars, keyboards and double bass, Clannad went on to become international best-sellers. As have two of its solo spin-offs: Mary Brennan and, perhaps more sensationally, her sister Enya. Enya's atmospheric, ethereal and painstakingly crafted albums, such as 1995's *The Memory of Trees*, have become synonymous with the Nineties' New Age aesthetic, and

IRISH MUSIC IS AS MUCH ABOUT SELF-EXPRESSION AS
IT IS ABOUT STYLE, WARMTH AND MUSICIANSHIP

have sold millions around the world.

Irish music is as much about self-expression as it is about style, warmth and musicianship. The sheer accessibility of music all over the country has nurtured a love and respect for a multitude of genres and styles, and fostered an acknowledgement that a certain amount of crossover is always inevitable. Many Irish artists have maintained their popularity over decades; Christy Moore, for example, has said that longevity comes from expressing deep feelings in your work. The Corrs' lyrical eloquence is matched by their musicianship and love of tradition. Add a contemporary sound and a modern outlook, and you've got a band who will endure in the years to come.

Traditional instruments

Tin Whistle – Andrea

Also called the penny whistle, this six-holed, keyless metal instrument is a cousin of the wooden flute. Although anyone can get a note from a tin whistle, it takes practice to perfect the embouchure (the mode of application of the lips) required to produce the wide variety of textures and clear flow of notes. Until 30 years ago, the tin whistle was viewed as the poor member of the woodwind family, inferior to both the uillean pipes and the flute. Then Ireland's Mary Bergin came along, exploring new keys and setting new standards, thus revolutionising the way the instrument was regarded. Her classic 1976 album *Feadoga Stain* was one of the first full-length recordings of tin whistle music ever released.

Andrea Corr takes the tin whistle a step further. Onstage, for example, the amplified whistle takes on a character of its own. Andrea will wind herself around a mic stand while playing, or beat out the rhythm with her stilettos, or – fingers flying – tilt the instrument down to the mosh pit, then up to the gods.

BODHRÁN – CAROLINE

The bodhrán is another Irish instrument which looks deceptively easy to play. Shaped like a large tambourine without the bells, it is a frame drum traditionally made of goatskin, but increasingly now of synthetic materials. It has a wooden rim on to which the skin is fixed by rivets, and is played either with the back of the hand or with a 'tipper'. This small double-ended drumstick is fatter on its two ends and thinner in the middle where it is held. Apart from tapping the skin, players also tap the stick on the wood and the rivets, which, especially when amplified by a contact microphone, creates a variety of effects.

Historically, the bodhrán can be linked to similar instruments in Norwegian and Arabian music. In Ireland it was originally used as a ritual instrument to accompany 'mummers' or 'wren boys' who went out revelling on December 26.

Now used to enhance and intensify the rhythm of a

WHEN PLAYING LIVE INSTRUMENTALS, CAROLINE WILL EMERGE FROM BEHIND HER DRUM KIT TO SIT CENTRE STAGE; HER BODHRÁN BALANCED ON HER LEFT KNEE, HER RIGHT HAND WORKING FURIOUSLY, HER HEAD BENT IN CONCENTRATION

session, the bodhrán didn't really come into its own until the great Sean O'Riada introduced it to mainstream traditional music in the 1960s, and The Chieftains continued his legacy. Today new styles of playing are constantly evolving.

Caroline's favourite bodhrán is inscribed with The Corrs' Celtic signature, and she plays it wearing her black golfing gloves with built-in grips. When playing live instrumentals, Caroline will emerge from behind her drum kit to sit centre stage; her bodhrán balanced on her left knee, her right hand working furiously, her head bent in concentration.

VIOLIN – SHARON

The violin becomes a 'fiddle' when used in Irish folk music. There is a broad geographical variation in the style of fiddle-playing across Ireland: the County Sligo style, for example, is ornate and showy; County Donegal fast-paced and melodic; County Clare slow and soulful. Fiddlers from the south west are famed for the polkas and slides (fast jigs) they perform for the local village dances, or 'sets'. Many of these styles have now fused, as bands have come together from disparate areas in search of commercial success.

Sharon's elastic violin playing fuels The Corrs' rhythmic fire. She has a favourite old acoustic fiddle, which she originally tried to adapt for use on stage by adding a pick-up. But for a larger, auditorium-worthy sound, she has ultimately found it easier to use a Barcus Berry jet-black electric violin when touring.

SHARON'S ELASTIC VIOLIN PLAYING FUELS THE CORRS' RHYTHMIC FIRE

UILLEAN PIPES

Played by Paddy Moloney on 'Little Wing', the uillean ('illun', or elbow) pipes are Ireland's answer to Scotland's bagpipes. Supplied with air by bellows held under the player's arm, the pipes produce a sensitive, distinctly Irish sound. They are comprised of a bag which stores the air, a nine-hole chanter with a two-octave range and a set of one-note drones. Regulators positioned on top of the drones allow the player – who is always seated – to provide the chords.

Uillean pipes arrived in Ireland in the 18th century from mainland Europe. They were beloved of both gentry and travellers, who played them in a restrained, parlour style and a flamboyant, ostentatious style respectively.

CAROLINE CORR

In December 1996, when Caroline Corr was back home in Dundalk for Christmas, she and some old friends visited the local disco – the same one she'd been going to for years. After dancing to a series of dancefloor classics, she was suddenly surprised when the DJ played 'Runaway' by The Corrs. Caroline, unable to reconcile her pop-star world with her real-life world, just stood there cringing. She has said that at the time she felt a bit like running away herself. Although she adores being part of one of the world's hottest musical acts, Caroline was having to get used to her two worlds colliding.

While not exactly shy and retiring, Caroline – according to friends and family – has become more outgoing since the band started. Coming across in interviews as having a personality somewhere in between the dramatic Andrea and the sophisticated Sharon, Caroline is thought to be the most serious Corr in terms of her career. Born on March 17 1973, this blue-eyed Corr is the second-youngest, and also the tomboy of the three girls. She jokes that photo shoots 'suck', and male journalists reckon she would be the most fun to take out on a night with the boys. Indeed, while Caroline was growing up in Dundalk most of her friends *were* boys.

Caroline likes people who are funny and charismatic, has admitted to a rather strange habit of pulling at her hair, and tends to confide in Andrea because she is the closest in age. With only 14 months between them, Caroline and Andrea shared a bedroom while growing up and were more or less raised as twins. She doesn't drive, is partial to the occasional bit of flirting and has said she simply couldn't do without her

mobile phone. She admires bands like Radiohead, The Verve and All Saints, and would like to see more girls out there making music.

She tries not to take to heart anything untrue or salacious written about The Corrs in the press, and takes what drooling male journalists say about The Corrs' sex appeal with a pinch of salt. Caroline believes strongly in mind over matter, and that if you want something enough you'll get it. Perhaps one of her weirdest traits is sniffing her jumper when sitting watching TV, a habit she laughingly explains performs the same function as a comforter. Caroline has only been playing the drums since 1993, but her musical accomplishments go way back. Her father Gerry taught her the piano, as he did all his kids, and Caroline very quickly mastered the instrument's technique. Caroline eventually gained a piano diploma, and briefly taught the instrument herself.

Caroline is proud of the Irish attitude towards music: most Irish parents believe it is important that their children play an instrument. She likes the fact that you seldom hear recorded music if you go out for a drink, as the pubs usually harbour a few traditional musicians of exemplary skill who love nothing more than an old-fashioned, spontaneous 'session'. Many of these musicians are shy people who express themselves through the hope and sadness of the music, and who can be entirely unaware of their virtuosity.

While continuing to take it in turns with her brother and sisters to play and practise on the piano, Caroline took up playing the bodhrán with a passion at an early age. The Corr household wasn't always filled with harmony, however; plenty of fights and hair-pulling went on between the girls. They have said that families have a way of knowing exactly how to tap into each other's insecurities, but these days The Corrs don't flare up at each other as much as they used to. After playing together in a band for so long, Caroline now considers them such a solid unit that, musically, even if one of them wasn't required to play a part, everyone would still be present. This united family front acts as a buffer against the pressures of touring. Caroline has remarked that as none of them have gone mad yet, it's highly unlikely that they ever will!

As a teenager Caroline played keyboards in the as-yet-unnamed band she'd formed along with her brother and sisters. Early video footage depicts a long-haired Caroline standing studiously behind her keyboard, or taking time out to giggle and swivel her hips in exaggerated movements. Caroline remembers that they rehearsed constantly, as if for

The Corr household wasn't always filled with harmony – plenty of fights and hair-pulling went on between the girls

 some imaginary major performance. Perfectionists all, they would practise endlessly in Jim's dank bedroom studio until they got their songs exactly right. She has said that all this manic hard work helped give The Corrs the discipline and stamina that is demanded of them today.

Caroline was still attending Dun Lughaidh Convent when the fledgling Corrs auditioned for Alan Parker's *The Commitments*. After a blink-and-you'll-miss-her cameo role in the film, Caroline went back to her bodhrán and piano. A year or so later, at the age of 18, a boyfriend and neighbour showed her a few basic beats on his drum kit. Caroline was hooked. She practised until she felt confident enough to invite Jim, Sharon and Andrea around for a private view; they all decided that they had found the drummer they were looking for – and the fact that she was their sister was a bonus.

A decidedly male domain, there have been few famous female drummers. Maureen 'Mo' Tucker from 1960s New York underground phenomenon The Velvet Underground, Patty Schemel of US guitar band Hole and the late Karen Carpenter stand out among the very few examples.

Male journalists reckon she would be the most fun to take out on a night with the boys

Caroline learned loops from teach-yourself CDs, and practised incessantly until she eventually became good enough to play in the band. For technical advice she took a few lessons from a respected Dundalk drumming teacher, but by this stage The Corrs were on the road. Practice was going to have to make perfect. Caroline had no trouble switching from the bodhrán to the drums, as both use the same rhythmic patterns, but what she

When touring, Caroline keeps fit by jogging, or using the gym facilities of the innumerable hotels

did find difficult was the physical strain that playing put on her hands. After drumming for four or five nights in a row, she discovered that the drumsticks were bruising her hands and giving her blisters. She wasn't sure how to tape them properly and still play to her exacting standards.

Caroline's hands would have toughened up eventually, but she decided on a immediate solution and bought a pair of black golfing gloves with in-built grips, which have since become her trademark. She now uses Yamaha drums when touring, and her bodhrán solos have become a highlight of The Corrs' live shows. On instrumentals such as 'Haste to the Wedding' and 'Toss the Feathers', Caroline emerges from behind her drum kit, bodhrán in hand, and dances down to the front of the stage to play. Sitting slightly forward on a chair, her face the picture of concentration, she deftly wields her stick, or 'tipper', variously on the instrument's skin, wood and rivets. The bodhrán responds with low and high notes, and an in built microphone adds body to the insistent rhythms.

On stage, she can give the bodhrán similar tones to a drum kit; for example, a high pitched sound which corresponds with the snare drum, and a low pitched sound which is similar to the kick drum. Caroline loves to experiment, and continues to elicit new sounds from the instrument.

In some instances, Caroline isn't required to play any instrument at all. When The Corrs appeared alongside Pavarotti at a War Child benefit in his home town of Modena, they sang an Italian folk song, *O surdato 'nnammurato*, standing sans instruments in front of two mike stands. Caroline says it was quite a daunting task to stand there and sing with 'The Maestro', especially since they were still learning their lines moments before going on stage. Naturally, they pulled it off with aplomb. Jim and Sharon shared

She hopes still to be making music in ten years' time, although she has confessed that marriage and babies will also become a priority down the line

one microphone, Andrea and Caroline another. The energy in Pavarotti's voice, Caroline has said, cannot be fully appreciated until you are standing beside him.

Caroline enjoys jamming with other traditional Irish musicians: in 1997, when The Corrs played an outdoor concert in Millstreet, County Cork on the 150th anniversary of 'Black 47' (the worst year of the Great Potato Famine), they were joined onstage by the renowned County Clare accordionist and fiddle player Sharon Shannon. Caroline found the experience 'exhilarating'.

When seated behind her kit, Caroline wears a headset with a microphone attached, like Janet Jackson and Madonna, which allows her to bash the drums and cymbals and simultaneously sing those harmonious backing vocals. The exertion she puts into her playing is palpable. She has said that it can sometimes cause soreness in her back, but she appreciates the strength it has given to her arms. For The Corrs' live shows, she'll often wear a black top and trousers, gold eyeshadow and, occasionally, a beauty spot applied with glitter. She'll clap her hands over her head and incite the crowd to clap along with her, and isn't averse to the odd drum roll as a final flourish.

When touring, Caroline keeps fit by jogging, or by using the gym facilities of the innumerable hotels. She likes to have fun, too: when recording *Forgiven, Not Forgotten* at

David Foster's expansive Malibu home, she would often be seen driving Foster's white golf buggy around the property, Jim perched – whooping and hollering – on the back. Caroline, who had her long hair cut into a chic, shorter style after completing The Corrs' first album, has said she feels certain that success hasn't changed any of them – a statement verified by their old friends in Dundalk. The only thing that has changed, she has said, is people's perceptions.

Like the other Corrs, she attributes much of their success to sheer hard work. For the time being, selling more records and reaching more people with their music is what her life is all about. She hopes still to be making music in ten years' time, although she has confessed that marriage and babies will also become a priority down the line. When The Corrs first burst into the public eye, Caroline, like Andrea and Jim, had little time and inclination for a boyfriend. She would have liked to go out for the occasional romantic candlelit dinner, but said she was happy to make such sacrifices for the sake of the band. In the interim she has managed to sustain a two year relationship with a property developer named Frank – a man willing to jump on a plane if that's what it takes to see her.

Sometimes Caroline dreams of doing little else but sitting on the sofa with a cup of tea, watching *Eastenders*. It's what she likes to do when she does get home to Dundalk (when time permits she hopes to buy a flat in Dublin with Andrea), often taking her phone off the hook and then heading out to catch up with old friends.

Though she appreciates the varied and interesting tasks required by the music industry – for example, recording albums, creating songs, making videos, doing photo shoots and playing live on stage in front of thousands of people – she is determined to keep her feet firmly planted on the ground. The real Caroline and the made-up, styled Caroline in the photographs can often seem to her like two different people entirely.

Still, Caroline is aware that image management is vital to The Corrs' profile. All The Corrs know that their public image can become distorted by untruths, and what irks Caroline most are accusations implying that because of the way The Corrs look, their musicianship and integrity must be lacking. 'It's a mistake to think we have no conviction in what we do,' she told *Q* magazine. 'There are people who say, three good-looking girls and their brother, nice family, writing nice songs, it's not serious. But if we all had torn jeans and greasy hair and didn't look so pretty, the expectations would be different, and perhaps we would be different people. We can only be what we are. That is, after all, what integrity is about.'

THE ALBUMS

In January, 1995, The Corrs set off to record *Forgiven, Not Forgotten* at Chartmaker, David Foster's studio in Malibu. Living in this haven of music (as The Corrs christened it), it took them five months to get it right. Jim was elated when Foster asked him to co-produce their debut album, as he admits he had been slightly worried that Foster might take the band too far down his road, diluting The Corrs' traditional Irish sound in the process. In fact, Foster was aware of the danger of such pitfalls. The great producer actually favoured the more traditional Irish elements of the recordings over the overtly American feel he had previously applied to tracks by artists such as Michael Jackson, Celine Dion and Whitney Houston. He had stated that if the finished product sounded completely different to The Corrs' demo recordings, then he would have failed in what he had set out to do.

As it turned out, the finished product and the demos were very similar. Foster merely added his expertise: his trademark lush string arrangements and dramatic finishes, for example, and the uncanny ability to bring out the best in vocalists. The Corrs have said that Foster had a way of energising their vocal harmonies so that their voices became three-dimensional. They were additionally aided by Bob Clearmountain, who they called 'the best mixer in the world', a man who has worked with artists including Bruce Springsteen, Tina Turner and The Rolling Stones. The Corrs have said that they don't know how much making their debut CD cost them, but imagined it was a substantial sum indeed.

Their fifteen track debut album *Forgiven, Not Forgotten* offers a polished, representative mix of The Corrs' versatile sound, from haunting traditional Irish instrumentals such as 'Erin Shore' and 'The Minstrel Boy' to straight-ahead, pop-rock tunes like 'Someday' and 'Love to Love You'. There's the Celtic reggae blend of 'The Right Time', tuneful ballads like 'Runaway' and to-the-point philosophical statements such as those on 'Closer'.

It was an album which sold by the million. In Ireland, for example, where it has gone an unprecedented nine times platinum, it is one of the all time best-selling debuts by a native recording group in the country's history. It made them megastars in Spain after a slow start. In the first four days after its release, 160 radio stations across America had played the single 'Runaway', which broke the record for a debut single from an Atlantic label. A joint Lava Records and 143 Records release (Foster and Jason Flom's Atlantic-distributed spin-off labels), *Forgiven, Not Forgotten* is a brilliant showcase of a talented young band's imaginative music.

Why did it take five months to record? Andrea has said that because they are a family, moving to Malibu felt very much like they were moving house. In short, they settled in. In order to reach the studio every morning, which they could walk to from their purpose-built accommodation, they had to pass the swimming pool. Often they got no further. All four were constantly present in the studio even if one of them wasn't required to play at the time.

The Corrs admit to being a little bit naive in not knowing exactly who David Foster had worked with when they piled into the Hit Factory to see him. Now they are fully aware that having the David Foster name attached to a new band is the equivalent of a Grade A certificate in the dog-eat-dog music business. But they had only done about seven small gigs before going into Chartmaker to record *Forgiven, Not Forgotten*, and can be excused for their lack of international knowledge.

There was no pressure on them when they first started writing for *Forgiven, Not Forgotten*, so they therefore wrote freely and naturally. The Corrs tried to keep this organic feeling in mind when they approached *Talk On Corners*. They'd been touring the world for a year and a half, which had given them ample opportunity to experiment and express themselves, which in turn led to them writing more passionate, guitar-oriented songs. On the *Forgiven, Not Forgotten* tour they had approached some tracks from a different angle, making them more raw, and adding more emphasis to the live drums.

There was no pressure on them when they first started writing for *Forgiven, Not Forgotten, so they therefore wrote freely and naturally*

The change in direction was not conscious – it just happened. At the same time, however, they knew they had to take a risk and move their music a little further along. They were also listening to what other bands were doing, and decided, next time around, to try to be a little less reliant on technology.

Jim has also said they were afraid they might have left it a bit too long between the first album and the follow up, which was recorded in Dublin and in Los Angeles in the summer of 1997, and released in October of that year. The main reason was because *Forgiven, Not Forgotten* kept taking off in various places all over the world, which meant The Corrs wanted to visit each territory, thus delaying the writing and recording of *Talk On Corners*.

Due to prior commitments, the in-demand David Foster was unable to produce the whole album and was only directly involved in four of the songs. But since he knew The Corrs and their work, and thoroughly enjoyed collaborating with

them on *Forgiven, Not Forgotten*, he made sure he was there at the helm. The Corrs have said it was an honour to be working with him again.

Talk On Corners took six months to complete. Being signed to a big American label more or less guarantees access to a variety of top notch writers and producers, and The Corrs happily took advantage. Production duties were spread around no less than seven different hit-making studio producers. Oliver Leiber, son of the legendary Jerry who co-wrote some of Elvis Presley's legendary early hits, co-wrote and produced tracks including the album's first single, the epic power ballad 'Only When I Sleep'. The Corrs also worked with Glen Ballard (who discovered and produced Alanis Morrisette), Rick Nowels, Billy Steinberg and David Foster himself. The Corrs' manager John Hughes produced the final track 'Little Wing', while Jim Corr himself produced 'What Can I Do', and co-produced the instrumental 'Paddy McCarthy' with the Ireland-based Leo Pearson.

The Corrs worked in each producer's studio, from the familiar surrounds of David

Foster's Chartmaker studio at Malibu (or 'Disneyland', as Sharon calls it) to Leo Pearson's in Dublin. Due to the pressures of touring, the band had only found the time and energy to write a couple of new songs, 'No Good For Me' and 'So Young' (for which Sharon had penned the lyrics), so they decided to collaborate on the songwriting as well. This time around, Andrea took on a much larger role, writing or co-writing most of the songs and evolving her songwriting skills in the process. Her collaborators included Leiber, Ballard and the legendary Carole Bayer Sager.

The songs on *Talk On Corners* continue to marry the traditional Irish influence with pop and rock. Jim has said that when The Corrs are writing a song they know instantly whether it is going to work with the addition of traditional music, and they never add the traditional sound just for the sake of it. The traditional music on *Talk On Corners* is less pervasive than it is on *Forgiven, Not Forgotten* – which does, after all, contain six instrumental tracks. While maintaining the Irish flavour, The Corrs' second album has a

more adventurous, cosmopolitan and hard-edged feel. They have said they feel it is a mature, expressive recording, heavy on good melodic lines and strong lyrics.

The Corrs progression was an organic one. When they went into the studio to record *Forgiven, Not Forgotten* they hadn't had much live experience at all, but they had just finished a huge world tour when they started on *Talk On Corners*. Naturally enough, they wanted to incorporate this live feel into their second album. They had grown to express their emotions onstage without a shred of self-consciousness, and they didn't want this new edge to be lost on record.

It also helped that some of the people they worked with, such as Oliver Leiber, were guitarists – which helped this 'edginess' develop naturally. Ultimately, though, The Corrs just decided to try new things, partly by matching up with other people. They found the whole experience great fun.

Andrea has admitted that they felt under tremendous pressure to impress with their new album after the first album did so well. The Corrs all tried to put these worries to the back of their minds, and concentrated on harnessing the positive, organic changes they'd experienced from touring. Jim has admitted that the radio-friendly, guitar-driven sound of *Talk on Corners* evolved partly in response to their fear of being labelled too middle-of-the-road. They also wanted to do something new, while simultaneously staying in tune with what their fans expected. They were worried, nevertheless; Caroline has confessed that they all thought their new, poppier sound might not go down so well in Ireland. But then they were also concerned that the music purists might take umbrage at the way they incorporated traditional influences into *Forgiven, Not Forgotten* – when, as it turned out, they loved it.

The Corrs need not have fretted over the Irish response to *Talk On Corners.* Launched

THE CORRS' SECOND ALBUM HAS A MORE ADVENTUROUS, COSMOPOLITAN AND HARD-EDGED FEEL

at a special event at Dublin's Lutrellstown Castle on 16 October 1997, it went straight in at number one on the first week of its release, and straight into seventh place on the UK. It went gold or platinum in 12 markets around the world, and in June 1998 peaked at number one in the UK album charts.

The song responsible for their breakthrough success in the UK was their version of Fleetwood Mac's 'Dreams', written by the latter's lead singer Stevie Nicks. The Corrs were asked to do a cover of 'Dreams' for the Fleetwood Mac tribute album *Legacy: Rumours Revisited*, after drummer and co-founder Mick Fleetwood heard their music and asked them to contribute. They don't feel that they have compromised in any way by doing cover versions, arguing that if it takes a cover song to break them into a market, so be it, as this will lead to increased interest in the rest of their music.

'Dreams' received such universal acclaim they decided to release it as a single. The reluctance of Britain's Radio One to give The Corrs airplay was laid to rest after the band employed the services of Chicago house DJ, producer and remixer Todd Terry to give 'Dreams' his special treatment. In May, 1998, he transformed The Corrs' already superlative version of 'Dreams' into a dancefloor smash, and helped take it high in the UK charts as a result.

The video for 'Dreams' was filmed in Singapore on one of the hottest, most humid days of the year. They spent eight hours in front of the cameras in the grounds of the Tlan Kok Seng Buddhist temple in Telok Ayer. Many bottles of Perrier and Evian were drunk throughout the proceedings, and Andrea kept her top unzipped at the back to help keep perspiration at bay!

The Corrs are perfectionists, who have to be totally happy with a product before they can OK it. Though delighted with *Talk On Corners*, they still felt it wasn't right for the American market. They went back to the studio, added more guitars, and America loved the result.

For those who dared to suggest that The Corrs didn't have full control over *Talk On Corners*, here's Andrea talking to Ireland's *Hot Press*: 'No-one else dictated terms on this album. The music went the way it should go. We all know music is a case of where business meets art, but no-one came along from the business side of things and told The Corrs "This is the way the song should be." If we allowed that to happen there is no way anyone on earth would be moved by the music we are creating. This album is a true expression of The Corrs, as we are now, in 1997. There is nothing on *Talk on Corners* that is dishonest. Every emotion was indulged!'

THE LYRICS

Just outside Dundalk, myths, legends and dramatic landscapes abound. St Brigid, Ireland's most revered saint after St Patrick, was reputedly born in Faughart, four kilometres north-east of Dundalk. Five kilometres to the north-west and balanced on a pinnacle of rock lies the 13th century Castleroche Castle, whose architect was thrown from a window to his death. Three kilometres north, the Giant's Load Proleek Dolmen is a Stone Age relic: a 47-tonne capstone balanced on three uprights. The pebbles scattered on its top are testament to the legend which promises a wish granted for every stone landed. Single women with good aim are purported to be married within the year.

Is it any wonder, then, that The Corrs' lyrics are steeped in love, life and tragedy; hope, dreams and fantasy? Andrea has said that their lyrics follow whatever the music inspires. Their highly polished songs are mainly concerned with love, but sometimes there is tragedy in the form of loss, as on the track 'Forgiven, Not Forgotten'. The latter touches on how it feels to have been involved with a man who killed himself, with the anguished narrator contemplating the same fate.

All The Corrs would rather allude to their subject matter rather than state it blatantly. Much of their lyrical subject matter is inspired by their own life experiences –

Where their

debut album

had a certain

homespun

innocence

about it, the

lyrics on *Talk*

On Corners

are more

vulnerable

and sensual

with no small measure of embellishment. Andrea the dreamer has said that she is inspired by tragedy, and that The Corrs' songs always contain enough depth to touch people's hearts. Written by Andrea, their hit single 'Runaway' obviously struck a chord with a lot of people. It articulates that all-consuming feeling of meeting someone you're so totally overwhelmed by you want to run away with them forever.

Where their debut album had a certain homespun innocence about it, the lyrics on *Talk On Corners* are more vulnerable and sensual. It has taken Andrea a few world tours to find the confidence to say the things she wanted to say without feeling self-conscious singing them in front of her family. All The Corrs have slowly let go of their inhibitions since they started songwriting, and have included substantially more passion in the later songs. Andrea still maintains, however, that tracks like 'When He's Not Around' and 'No Good For Me' are the product of imagination and fantasy.

Talk On Corners takes its title from a line in the song 'Queen of Hollywood', which Andrea wrote with Glen Ballard about a girl's dreams of conquering the silver screen. And if people think it's about her own screen ambitions, they're wrong. It's just a song for dreamers, she has said, and Andrea is definitely one of those.

ANDREA CORR

Born on May 17 1974, brown-eyed Andrea Jane Corr is the group's charismatic lead singer and tin whistle player, a woman who oozes star quality both on- and offstage. Andrea says her best musical experience so far was playing in front of 20,000 people in an open air concert on the west coast of Ireland, and hearing everyone sing the songs back to her. She works out at the gym, wears spectacles or contact lenses, doesn't have a driving licence and has a bad habit of losing things – which is why she counts the inexpensive tin whistle as her perfect instrument! Of all the band members, she has the messiest room. Like Sharon, Andrea is an eternal optimist, a trait which she reckons can get a bit wearing at times, and one she puts down to the naturally sunny nature of the Irish. Her wicked sense of humour frequently makes the others crack up with laughter. She believes firmly in the do-as-you-would-be-done-by precept of karma, and is attracted to people who are down to earth and live life to the full.

Between sound checks and performances, on tour buses and planes, and even – if she's not too exhausted – in bed after a show, Andrea likes to read, usually with her thumb in her mouth as she does so. Her thumb-sucking is a lifelong habit which her family hardly notice anymore; others, however, do. A concerned member of the music business pulled John Hughes aside during a US visit in 1998, and suggested that he encourage Andrea to consider therapy as a cure. Andrea, who hasn't a problem with her rather endearing trait, found the idea absolutely hilarious.

In keeping with her reputation as the group's romantic dreamer, one of her favourite authors is the magic realist Gabriel Garcia Marquez. With thumb in mouth and Garcia Marquez novel on lap, Andrea can disappear into a fantasy world of her own – something she is likely to do even when she isn't reading. The Corrs' main lyricist has often ascribed the motivation behind her songs to her overactive imagination, if only for privacy's sake. She might share her life more or less full-time with her brothers and sisters, but there are still certain things she doesn't want them to know.

The baby of the family, it was taken as read that Andrea would learn the piano, as Jim, Sharon and Caroline had done before her. She has joked in interviews that their parents actually locked them in the piano to keep them quiet. Blessed with extraordinary beauty and an equally extraordinary singing voice, the youngest Corr accrued confidence and maturity at an early age. She also acted in a handful of school plays at Dundalk's Dun Lughaidh convent, which might have helped.

Although she toyed with the idea of going on to university, her real love was music. She was determined to make it as a singer. As they were growing up, Andrea and Caroline shared a bedroom they'd plastered with posters of their teen idols Nik Kershaw, Prince and Depeche Mode, and all the girls would pop round the corner to Jim's house to rehearse for a stardom that was still very much a dream.

Those auditions for *The Commitments* helped turn this dream into reality. Footage of fifteen-year-old Andrea speaking to camera reveals a pretty, obliging young adult with long, permed hair, telling the film's casting agents that yes, it was the first time The Corrs had come together as a band. Charmed, they cast Andrea in a small role as Jimmy Rabbitte's sister Sharon; and the film's musical advisor John Hughes simultaneously decided to manage the group. At the time, Andrea was a much more frenetic dancer than the fluid but composed image she now presents. Captured on home video, she wiggles wildly around in a tiny pair of leather trousers, her face a picture of ambition and determination.

Today the perfectly mannered Andrea cringes on remembering some of the lines the foul-mouthed Sharon Rabbitte had to say, although she'll laugh on recalling the scene where she was filmed brushing her big curly mop of hair in front of a mirror. She obviously did something right, for Alan Parker, the film's director, kept this beautiful colleen in mind for future roles. In 1996, when the time came for him to direct the film version of the rock opera *Evita*, he cast Andrea as Juan Peron's teenage mistress.

She has joked

in interviews

that their

parents

actually

locked them

in the piano

to keep

them quiet

Andrea's co-stars included Jonathan Pryce as Peron, Antonio Banderas as Che Guevara and, as the eponymous heroine, Madonna. Written by Andrew Lloyd Webber and Tim Rice, the entire script was sung.

Parker was so keen on having Andrea Corr in his film that he adjusted Madonna's shooting schedule to accommodate her. The Corrs had just finished a three-week tour, taking in four continents in the process, and while the others went back home to Ireland for a rest, John Hughes and Andrea Corr flew to Budapest for her day's shooting. Andrea has admitted that, in the months prior to filming, she was extremely anxious about her small role. But when it came to the crunch, tour fatigue overwhelmed her nerves and she just went in there and performed her intense, poignant scene to the best of her ability.

Many headlines ensued about Andrea being thrown out of bed by Madonna. In the scene, Madonna walks into the room where Peron and his young mistress are lying, and sings the song 'Hello and Goodbye' before kicking Andrea out on the street. Andrea takes her suitcase, wondering (in song) what will happen and where she is meant to go, and leaves. As Evita, Madonna was so necessarily cold in that scene that she later came up to Andrea and apologised. She added that she was a big fan of The Corrs' music, and Andrea naturally accepted her apology.

Andrea's long, curly hair in *Evita* is a wig. She'd had her hair cut shorter after The Corrs began to take off; Alan Parker had remembered her as the girl with the unruly curly perm from *The Commitments*. He quickly arranged for wardrobe to lengthen her locks so she looked what he considered to be typically Argentinean.

Acting is only a sideline for Andrea, who considers the band and its music her number one priority. She always anticipated The Corrs' success, but acting isn't something she has actively pursued. Luck brought it to her instead. The Corrs view their lead singer's thespian career as healthy because it increases public awareness of their music. For Sharon, Andrea's aptitude for acting is commensurate with her role as lead singer, as it is lead singers who usually tend to have dramatic personalities. Indeed, The Corrs have fondly referred to the sassy Andrea as 'the drama queen of the family.'

An incurable romantic, Andrea will often make more out of a situation than actually exists. She believes in the stories she weaves as a lyricist, and is prepared to look deep into the feelings they represent. For example, though the tragic suicide alluded to in 'Forgiven, Not Forgotten' had no basis in Andrea's reality, she likened writing such subject matter to an emotional rollercoaster. She has said that she related to the feeling of emptiness evoked in 'When He's Not Around', as she had once been very attracted to a married man and exaggerated the situation in her imagination.

Although she's now used to pouring her emotions into her singing, the good Catholic girl used to worry what her parents and siblings would think of her song lyrics. But after going from pub gigs to playing stadia around the world, Andrea is no longer the ingenue who, on that first flight to Boston, couldn't believe there was free food on board. These days her sensuality has come to the fore in her songs and her peformance. As all the girls began to express themselves more on stage, they also began to dress accordingly. Andrea is always sleekly and elegantly dressed (even when wearing a clumpy pair of Dr Marten's boots), a few strands of hair often falling over her face for full sultry effect, a trio of diamond studs in her right ear, her nails painted dark blue, a single ring on the middle finger of her right hand. She's a charismatic live performer, with a clear, rich voice and a charming tendency to lose herself in the music.

Whether tousling her hair as if unsure of what to do with her hands, crouching forward imploringly or holding her face to indicate a lover's caress, curling herself around the mike stand to play her tin whistle, running up stairs to stand on a platform high above Caroline on drums, or even simply raising one quizzical eyebrow, Andrea flirts with her audiences – and wins everyone over in the process. Her relaxed intimacy could be likened to that of the old time Irish traditional singers. Smiling, laughing, pouting, smouldering and blowing kisses into the auditorium, she expresses a gamut of emotional states.

Because Andrea went straight from school into The Corrs, it is often said that she, more than any of the others, missed out on the chance to lead a normal life. Andrea has answered that she feels she is gaining more than she is missing, and feels incredibly lucky. The one thing missing from her life is a boyfriend, although she feels this will be remedied when she eventually decides that she wants to settle down. Andrea the fantasist has said that when she is attracted to someone, she is equally attracted to the inevitable tragic side of the romance, and reckons that where there is love there is pain.

She even tries to see the more mundane and domestic aspects of relationships through rose-coloured glasses. When touring with Celine Dion, for example, it transpired that both women shared a passion for dishwashing and housework, probably because it makes them feel grounded after months on the road.

Andrea eschews the 'feminist' tag in favour of being feminine, beautiful and powerful. She would never kiss a man she didn't want to kiss, or dally with someone who

SHE ADMITS
THAT FAME
HAS MADE
HER SLIGHTLY
SHYER AND
MORE
CAUTIOUS
OF MEN

was already in a relationship. She acknowledges that she is attractive, but stresses that it is an attractiveness that comes mostly from her heart and soul.

Ultimately, although she admits that fame has made her slightly shyer and more cautious of men, Andrea plans to get married and have babies. Tagged 'the sexiest woman in Ireland' by one Irish newspaper, and as the object of desire for millions of male fans, it's easy to think of Andrea as inundated with suitors. Indeed, many a marriage proposal has been yelled out to Andrea at The Corrs' live shows. Even the former *Coronation Street* pin-up turned-singer, Matthew Marsden, and the presenter of the *O-Zone*, Jamie Theakston, have publicly revealed their crushes on her. But the tightly knit nature of The Corrs, combined with the fact that any time off Andrea gets is spent with family and old friends, has meant dates are rare. Andrea, who still lives at home with her parents, has confessed that she hasn't had a relationship in years.

Still, she continues to dream. She gets very emotional watching movies, considering them the perfect medium in which to explore the same emotions she likes to write about

in her songs. Favourite films include *Leaving Las Vegas*, *The Piano* and *Midnight Cowboy*. Plus *The Commitments* and *Evita*, of course.

Andrea might not be able to watch herself in Warner Brothers' first fully animated film, 1998's *The Quest For Camelot*, but she can certainly hear her voice. In this cartoon story about King Arthur's search for the magic sword Excalibur, Andrea Corr is the singing voice of Kayley, the King's daughter. The film's soundtrack features two new songs sung by Andrea and penned by David Foster and Carole Bayer Sager: 'On My Father's Wings', and a duet with country music legend Bryan White, 'Looking Through Your Eyes'.

Andrea has said she is immensely proud of The Corrs' success, especially because they haven't compromised to get where they are today. Instead of taking the traditional route of playing anywhere, just in the hope they would get noticed, The Corrs quietly concentrated on amassing a decent range of material that they could take to a record company. She is grateful in retrospect that their first single, 'Forgiven, Not Forgotten', wasn't a world-wide hit, as back then they might not have been able to handle becoming megastars overnight.

Andrea has a free-spirited attitude to success, and likes to think that she is being guided in whatever she does, and that whatever will be, will be. Still, it doesn't stop her – or the rest of them – being extremely self-critical. As their father Gerry told *Hot Press* in

Andrea has said she is immensely proud of The Corrs' success, especially because they haven't compromised to get where they are today

August 1996, 'They were playing at the launch of the European presidency in Temple bar last week but we recorded it on video as well. When the children came home Andrea was the first to watch it and she was going, "Oh my God, I was awful." You know, looking for every little flaw, every tiny mistake.

Gerry has added that it's a rare occurrence when Andrea likes hearing something she has sung. Apparently none of The Corrs have yet reached the stage where they can relax and admit they are pop stars. Nevertheless, Andrea philosophically concedes that they are all lucky people who should appreciate what they have.

While refusing to do sensationalist interviews out of principle and because such interviews would impinge on the other band members and their manager, Andrea also feels a certain responsibility to more vulnerable fans who could be swayed by her opinions. She is firmly opposed to drug use, and chastises rock stars for making the practice seem glamorous to the young and impressionable.

Sometimes, Andrea has said, people in the music industry seem little more than clowns, and in such an environment she often feels like a caricature. While not averse to a bit of glamour herself, there are times when she simply wants to scrub off all her make-up and run away. But as long as she remains intact and happy, Andrea intends to front The Corrs for a good while yet.

✝ Touring
✝he World

When *Forgiven, Not Forgotten* was released in October 1995, The Corrs' lifestyle changed in a way that was to set the standard for the years that followed: they began touring the world. Being signed to a major American label meant that their product would be distributed all over the globe, and The Corrs knew that – as debut artists – they would have to work hard to ensure that each territory got to appreciate them. Their first world tour began in Ireland – in Ennis, County Clare, to be precise – and continued into other European countries. It expanded to take in Canada, America, Australia and South East Asia, finishing up in Tokyo, Japan.

In a very short space of time they went from playing to an audience of 250 in an Irish club, to opening for such stars as Celine Dion in Scotland in front of 10,000 people. At the Odense Festival in Denmark they played in front of 35,000 people; at London's Fleadh Festival at Finsbury Park they shared the bill with Sting and The Chieftains and won over a crowd of 50,000.

However large or small the venue, it was an unremitting schedule which, for two and a half years, often saw them gigging day in, day out. Sometimes it was easy for them to forget what country they were in – the cliché 'if it's Tuesday, it must be Belgium' was a fitting one to apply to the blur of hotels, venues, radio stations, press conferences and promotional appearances The Corrs whizzed through morning, noon and night.

While touring Germany, for example, they were also obliged to perform in five other European countries in one week. They turned up and delivered superlative shows in each, before jetting back to Germany to take up where they left off. On 18 May 1996, they flew in from Amsterdam to sing at Dublin's Rugby Peace International event at Lansdowne

Road, a match between Ireland and the Barbarians, organised by the Peace International group. As soon as the event finished four hours later they were chauffeured off to the airport to continue their tour in Copenhagen.

At the time, a weary but smiling Andrea joked that she was never one for public transport. There was no respite even once aboard the plane: it was full of competition winners who got to fly to Denmark and see The Corrs in concert. The bonus prize was that they got to chat to The Corrs all the way there as well – a deal with which the band complied graciously.

Being a warm-hearted bunch who are genuinely interested in other people, The Corrs seize every opportunity to find out a little about each place they visit. Andrea will always greet each audience with a few words in their own language, to wild cheering and thunderous applause. They'll all try the local delicacies and see the sights if time permits. Jim can usually be spotted in the small hours at a downtown nightclub; the girls will often pose for photos outside a local landmark or even with some of the native fauna, such as the koala Andrea was snapped with in Australia.

It is always intriguing to see whether a band who sound fabulous on record can cut it live. Especially a band such as The Corrs, who often play the kind of music that previously had belonged in noisy Irish pub sessions. Would they succeed in projecting it in arenas the size of small villages? The Corrs have proved without a shadow of a doubt that they are among the world's best live performers. Gregarious, gorgeous and eminently likeable, they write or co-write their own songs, are blessed with sublime singing voices and the ability to play their own instruments (it's no secret that many of today's superstars have never penned a lyric, let alone picked up a guitar) – in short, they are everything a band should be.

Andrea has said that playing live is one of the most important things a musician can do. The effect is threefold: the band members can all see and interact with each other, they are expressing themselves and shaking off any inhibitions, and they can clearly see the effect their music is having on their audience. It has, she has also said, transformed them as people. Constant touring has given them more confidence and an edgier, rockier sound. When the time came to record *Talk On Corners*, they brought this fresh attitude with them.

The Corrs have recruited two extra musicians for their live shows, more often than not Keith Duffy on bass guitar and Anto Drennan on electric guitar. For The Corrs' legion of fans, these two are inevitably outsiders; The Corrs, however, think of them as two additional members of

ANDREA HAS SAID THAT PLAYING LIVE IS ONE OF THE MOST IMPORTANT THINGS A MUSICIAN CAN DO

the family. Anto Drennan has been a friend of Jim's since they played together in Dublin bands many years ago, and they auditioned and welcomed Keith Duffy after he was recommended to them. Anto's intense guitar solos have become a highlight during such tracks as 'Haste to the Wedding'. But for classics such as 'Little Wing', which they were already playing live before they recorded it with The Chieftains for *Talk On Corners*, they like to bring things down to an acoustic level.

The dynamism of *Talk On Corners* gave The Corrs an entirely new lease of life on stage. As the songs were more energetic, The Corrs became more energetic in performing them. Indeed, some of the more striking moments in their stage shows are when they bring everything down to acoustic instruments only, so that it is only the four Corrs (with Caroline on bodhrán) who are playing their instruments. Then, gradually, they raise the scale again so that the whole band joins in. Caroline will sprint back to behind her drum kit, and the auditorium will erupt with full-tilt rock once more.

For The Corrs, playing live is what they are all about. After a gig they will usually sit around and discuss its good and bad points, congratulating themselves on the material

which went down a storm and vowing to eradicate or tighten up any rare mistakes or loose spots. They have said that touring has been the best possible education, in that it's an exercise which pays huge creative dividends.

Still, there were times earlier on when they wondered whether it was all worth it. When performing to a handful of people in an under-publicised gig in France at the end of 1996, for example, they found themselves exhausted. Given the pressure they had been under and the constant strain of touring, all the girls broke down in tears. Nevertheless, after a rejuvenating Christmas break in Dundalk, they were back on the road again.

Touring can take its toll physically. Although they tried to take a break back home in Dundalk (or in Sharon's case, Belfast) every two or three months, by the end of 1997 they had all come down with flu and other assorted ailments. In the past, the surge of adrenalin they got from playing live has disguised the fact that they are ill or run down. Older and wiser, they now make sure they look after themselves by eating properly and working out regularly at a hotel gym, regardless of where they are. By tackling the whole world simultaneously, they nearly burnt themselves out. It was a learning experience. As well as planning to spend more time taking care of their health, The Corrs have vowed to play more shows in Britain in the future.

Nevertheless, they have said that they grew up a lot on that first tour. It made them realise how much they really hankered for success, and so they truly appreciated it when it arrived. They learnt that they still crave more and more success all over the world. They also learnt how important it is to spend some time apart from each other, in order for them to come back together refreshed and ready to face the next challenge. They have joked that it's not normal for siblings to still be together at their age, and love to sing Sister Sledge's 'We Are Family' during their live shows.

The Corrs have become a powerful attraction for people of Irish descent around the world, as well as for anyone who simply loves great music and great performances. Early on, their fans were generally a polite, quiet lot, who would sidle up to say hello and request an autograph. Now that they have shaken media hands in the UK, Europe, America, Canada, South East Asia, Australia, New Zealand and Latin America, their fan base – though still well mannered – has inevitably grown noisier. The biggest screamers are in Spain, where *Forgiven, Not Forgotten* suddenly went double platinum after a slow start, *Talk On Corners* went gold in one day, and they win more awards than U2 and Oasis.

The Corrs will always make time after their shows to meet fans, sign autographs and pose for photos. Accessibility is important to them, and they are flattered by the attention

The Corrs

have become

a powerful

attraction for

people of

Irish descent

around

the world

Being a warm-hearted bunch who are genuinely interested in other people, The Corrs seize every opportunity to find out a little about each place they visit

they get. They believe that having bodyguards only leads to a 'must get at them' way of thinking, so they don't have any. If any of them get a bit big-headed, they are always deflated by a trip home to Ireland, whose inhabitants have a habit of pretending not to notice famous people. It also means The Corrs can go down the pub and relax. They once encountered top Irish-Canadian family group the Barra MacNeils playing in a small pub in Dundalk, and Jim further endeared himself to The Corrs' multitudes of Canadian fans by later stating how much he admired their bodhrán player Lucy MacNeil's mastery of the instrument. They made a series of memorable appearances in their homeland in 1996, specifically at a televised gala in Temple Bar to celebrate Ireland's presidency of the European Union, and on the world's largest aircraft carrier, the US Navy's *JFK*, in Dublin Bay. The latter – a special Independence Day party for over 1,000 VIPs – was at the invitation of America's Irish ambassador Jean Kennedy Smith. The Corrs filmed the video for their single 'Love to Love You' on board, posed for pictures and climbed up to the bridge and control tower. For this performance the sound deck was placed between the wings of a fighter plane. Andrea momentarily lost her balance at one point, triggering a stampede of sailors hoping to set her upright again.

But the live performance that really changed The Corrs' fortunes was the one on 17 March, St Patrick's Day, 1998, at London's Royal Albert Hall. Broadcast on BBC1 in the UK on the same night, it was also shown at intervals (according to time zones) by the Odyssey Cable Network across the United States, attracting approximately 50 million American viewers. It seems strange to think that The Corrs had only played three London dates before they booked the 7000-seater on the advice of their agent, and that they were nervous that nobody would show. The place sold out, Mick Fleetwood turned up to guest on drums, and the UK's influential radio stations began playing their music almost overnight.

While it had taken The Corrs a while to crack the British and American markets, they were already superstars in South East Asia, where – despite a recession and problems with piracy – *Talk On Corners* was at the top of the recording industry's album charts for 30 weeks, spending eight weeks at Number One.

They have professed to be constantly amazed at the way their music is so avidly consumed in places such as Japan and Malaysia, putting its appeal down to the uniqueness of the traditional Irish elements in their pop/rock sound. Their biggest

The live

performance

that really

changed

The Corrs'

fortunes was

the one on

17 March,

St Patrick's Day

1998, at

London's Royal

Albert Hall

televised live performance yet – and indeed, perhaps ever – was at the closing ceremony for the Commonwealth Games in Kuala Lumpur, where they were a hit with an international crowd of spectators and athletes from over 70 countries. Their TV audience was a gargantuan 400 million; Jim has said that they could have relied on using a backing tape, but that nothing beats the adrenaline rush from singing live for that many people.

The Corrs in Australia

The Corrs consider Australia to be the country which kick-started their career. It is The Corrs' largest market outside Ireland, representing a third of their total music sales. Of the two million-plus copies sold internationally of *Forgiven, Not Forgotten*, 600,000 copies were sold in Australia, where it is also the sixth biggest-selling album in the history of Warner Music Australia. They have visited the continent four times, the last time in February 1998, and like to describe their national tours there as being like a holiday, or a home away from home. They have waxed rapturous about such attractions

as the Great Barrier Reef and the Sydney Opera House, and have always
said that in the unlikely event that things went wrong for them, they
could always move down under.

There has been a blitz of in-store appearances, sell out gigs and
photo-shoots in the blistering heat. The Corrs have visited Canberra's
Wannaissa High School as part of a celebration of Irishness, and
Sydney's Children's Hospital before playing the city's State Theatre –
Andrea being so moved that she decided (in an Aussie accent) to
christen their national dates the 'Go For Your Life' tour. Australian
audiences are apparently the hardest ones to keep in their seats during
a Corrs performance, and especially so during the instrumental
numbers.

The Corrs have attributed their success in the antipodes to a
combination of their record company's belief in them, their promo tours and the vast
number of people of Irish descent in Australia. Jim has said that Australians and Irish
have similar characteristics, in that they are both straight talkers who like to have fun,
and who enjoy relaxing with a few drinks.

Jim has made time to go diving off the Great Barrier Reef, and all The Corrs took a
holiday – together – on Queensland's tropical Hamilton Island. There they jetskiied, went
scuba diving and sailed out to a deserted island, all the while protecting their milky Irish

Even in bikinis and sunglasses the girls were recognised by fans, some of
whom had won a competition to 'Meet The Corrs on Hamilton Island'

complexions with large sunhats. Even in bikinis and sunglasses the girls were recognised
by fans, some of whom had won a competition to 'Meet The Corrs on Hamilton Island'.
The band also gave a private performance to 100 guests while they were there.

However, disaster nearly struck on their 1997 tour when manager John Hughes
decided to take a dip in the Pacific Ocean, blithely unaware of the strong undercurrents
that were lurking. Within minutes, he was swept so far out that he couldn't
see the coastline. Luckily he was spotted and rescued by a windsurfer. This
didn't dampen the band's enthusiasm for the country, and they indicated
their feelings on their last visit by bringing their parents along with them.

Britain, America and the Future

While the rest of the world couldn't get enough of The Corrs' Celtic pop rock, those two major music territories, Britain and America, were perplexingly slow to catch on to the group's obvious charms. The band already had a substantial following in these countries, but they wanted to hit the big time in both – success in Britain and America being a must for any band aspiring to be truly international. A variety of factors, not least the group's talent and tenacity, eventually overcame any resistance. The Corrs quest for what they jokingly refer to as 'world domination' is now becoming a reality.

The reasons behind their initial struggle in the United Kingdom are straightforward. Though 1995's *Forgiven, Not Forgotten* sold more than two million copies worldwide (and had The Corrs playing packed out stadia everywhere from Ireland to Indonesia on the back of it), it received little radio airplay in Britain. Territories such as Australia, Spain and Denmark, for example, had launched the album alongside TV, radio and poster campaigns, and The Corrs had headlined live shows.

Being signed to a major American label meant that The Corrs' debut album received worldwide distribution, and the group toured each territory accordingly. They would even double back and revisit a country if the album suddenly took off there, as was the case in Spain. A support slot for Celine Dion's world tour boosted sales even further – but not necessarily in the UK.

The Corrs were vexed. After all, they did grow up watching British bands on the BBC

television programme *Top of the Pops*, and were avid followers of the British music scene. Despite reaching number one in numerous places around the world, they hankered after a top spot in the UK.

Timing was important: when *Forgiven, Not Forgotten* had its UK release back in 1995, Britpop was all the rage. Guitar-oriented bands such as Blur, Pulp and Oasis were monopolising the record-buying market. Then there was techno, the synthetic, thumping house beat which was dominating Britain's clubs. At that time there didn't seem to be a place for The Corrs' melodic pop music with its traditional Irish strain. The Corrs, of course, didn't point their collective finger at anyone – they just set about writing stronger songs for their follow up, 1997's *Talk On Corners*.

Sharon has said that their image as a family band didn't help them much in Britain, either. Then there was the fact that they were Irish and played traditional Irish music, but also leant heavily on pop and rock. British record shops, with their mandatory categories for different types of music, simply didn't know which bracket to stick them in. In seemed that, in the UK, the very thing that made The Corrs unique was proving to be their nemesis.

John Hughes found himself faced with the same problem when he first set about trying to get the band signed to a label. The UK, America and even Ireland deemed them too folk for pop, and too pop for folk. Luckily, the faith of Jason Flom and David Foster helped The Corrs transcend the 'too difficult' tag, and the group went to vindicate their belief – everywhere except in Britain. And where the latter was then enthralled with Britpop, America was equally besotted with the grunge subculture coming from Seattle.

Nevertheless, just four days after its release, some 160 radio stations across the United States were playing the *Forgiven, Not Forgotten* single 'Runaway'. It was a record for a debut single from the Atlantic label. The Corrs bolstered this initial success by visiting many such stations (in some cases before they had even got the single at all) and playing an acoustic version in the studios. This led to a mini American tour of small acoustic venues in March, 1996. The Corrs have pointed out that they released in America first simply because they are signed to an American record label.

Finally, in 1998, The Corrs' determination to defy categorisation or marketing by demographics paid off. They had said that all they needed was to be heard in Britain, and that they wouldn't accept failure until they were. When they took the now legendary gamble of hiring the Royal Albert Hall, their wish came true. The concert, which was televised live in the UK and right across America, proved to be a turning point in their

Despite reaching

number one in

numerous places

around the world,

they hankered

after a top spot

in the UK

After their UK
chart success was
assured The
Corrs promised
to devote more
time to their
British audiences

international career. The Corrs have said that they felt the difference immediately during the UK gigs that followed the show.

Consequently the single, 'Dreams', began to receive heavy rotation on UK radio, but not, however, on the elusive Radio One. *Talk On Corners* re-entered the UK chart at number 14; by mid-June, after 30 weeks on the British charts, it finally hit number one. *Forgiven, Not Forgotten* belatedly went gold. Still determined to be played on Radio One, The Corrs got master remixer Todd Terry to work his magic on 'Dreams' – and suddenly Radio One loved the record! By this stage, the press were championing the foursome, which also raised awareness, and very soon The Corrs became a ubiquitous presence in the UK charts. By September, Jim was joking about how good it felt to be selling more records than their compatriots, Boyzone. By October, their next single 'What Can I Do' was receiving more than 1,700 plays a week on UK radio.

America had also been treated to The Corrs' Albert Hall performance, and 'Dreams' consequently rocketed into the US Top 40 in April 1998. In June they played all three dates – New York, Chicago and the San Francisco Bay Area – of the annual Guinness Fleadh roadshow, amidst a stellar line-up including Tracy Chapman, Sinead O'Connor and blues legend John Lee Hooker. In November 1998 they began a tour of the East Coast, taking in

In one of their online chats on the internet, The Corrs summed up their outlook in three words: positivity, compassion and empathy

Chicago, Washington, Philadelphia, Boston and New York City.

After their UK chart success was assured The Corrs promised to devote more time to their British audiences. True to their word, they kicked off their biggest ever UK tour in December 1998, playing over 25 dates around the country, taking in Glasgow, Cardiff, Newcastle and finishing up in Manchester. They also played two dates at the venue which symbolises success in Britain: the cavernous Wembley Arena. As with the rest of the tour, tickets for that venue sold out in a matter of hours.

In one of their online chats on the internet, The Corrs summed up their outlook in three words: positivity, compassion and empathy. It's a philosophy which reveals the integrity of a band who are determined to do things their way, without compromise or artifice. Their honesty is as essential a part of them as their music.

When asked if they would ever consider releasing a purely instrumental album, The Corrs have replied that they would love to score a film one day - which would obviously involve doing a lot of instrumentals. They will continue to remix and re-release the occasional old track, and previously unreleased numbers such as 'On Your Own' and even the early 'Make You Mine' may find their way onto forthcoming CD singles.

Big business is catching on to The Corrs' abundant charms: Britain's Lloyds TSB Bank, in an effort to capture the youth market, signed a long-term marketing deal with The

Corrs in late 1998. The bank will use a re-worded version of 'What Can I Do?' in a forthcoming advertising campaign.

After employing the services of such musical giants as Michael Jackson, Madonna, Tina Turner, the Spice Girls and Boyzone, multinational soft drink company Pepsi have confirmed the significance of The Corrs in the rock industry by signing the band for their 1999 advertising and promotion campaign. Another previously unreleased Corrs track, 'Love in the Milky Way', will feature in the first commercial in March, and Pepsi buyers will be able to acquire Corrs memorabilia and exclusive singles, and will have

Their idiosyncratic music has touched a chord the world over

opportunities to meet the band. True to form, The Corrs have said that they intend to use some of the money received from the deal to keep their concert ticket prices down.

The band continue to offer their services to causes close to their heart. In the past, for example, they have endorsed the *Ulster Daily Mirror*'s seatbelt campaign for drivers, and the Dublin-based Irish Music Expansion Scheme, which aims to raise one million pounds for new and merging Irish artists. It was Andrea Corr who organised a one-off benefit concert on RTE's *Late Late Show* on November 20 1998, for the victims of the Omagh bombing tragedy. In a symbolic statement that it would not be forgotten and should never happen again, Andrea rounded up The Corrs, U2, Bob Geldof, Paul Brady, Sharon Shannon and others to appear on the programme. The Corrs also feature on the Omagh charity album *Across the Bridge of Hope*, alongside Boyzone, Ash and U2.

The Corrs' popularity continues to skyrocket. Their videos dominate TV stations like MTV, and their music is a regular fixture of radio playlists around the world. Their live shows sell out rapidly and provide an unforgettable spectacle for the millions who attend. Yet there is never even a glimpse of the huge egos that often come with superstardom.

The Corrs continue to be the polite and humble individuals they were brought up to be, ensuring that interviewers come away smitten and fans in their millions keep clamouring to hear and see them. Their idiosyncratic music has touched a chord the world over.

Discography

As befits a truly international band, The Corrs' music has been released in different forms at varying times in many countries around the world. The dates and catalogue numbers below refer to material released in the UK and throughout Europe.

Singles

1995
The Right Time
7567-95680-2

Runaway
7567-95733-2

1996
Forgiven, Not Forgotten
7567-95687-2

Love To Love You
7567-95621-2

1997
Only When I Sleep
7567-84017-2

I Never Loved You Anyway
7567-84045-2

1998
What Can I Do
7567-84063-2

Dreams
7567-84113-2

So Young
7567-844162

Albums

1995
Forgiven, Not Forgotten
7567-92612-2
Erin Shore/Forgiven, Not Forgotten/Heaven Knows/Along With The Girls/Someday/Runaway/The Right Time/The Minstrel Boy/Toss The Feathers/Love To Love You/Secret Life/Carraroe Jig/Closer/Leave Me Alone/Erin Shore

1997
Talk On Corners
7567-83051-2/7567-83106-2 (re-release)
Only When I Sleep/When He's Not Around/What Can I Do/I Never Loved You Anyway/So Young/Don't Say You Love Me/Love Takes Love Gives/Hopelessly Addicted/Paddy McCarthy/Intimacy/Queen Of Hollywood/No Good For Me/Little Wing

Videos

1998
The Corrs Live at the Royal Albert Hall
7567-80871-3
When He's Not Around/No Good For Me/Love To Love You/Forgiven, Not Forgotten/Joy Of Life/Intimacy/What Can I Do/The Right Time/Queen Of Hollywood/Dreams/Haste To The Wedding (Parts 1 & 2)/Runaway/Only When I Sleep/Hopelessly Addicted /I Never Loved You Anyway/So Young/Toss The Feathers